IMPROVING COMMUNICATION

AN ESSENTIAL GUIDE FOR COUPLES

Roy & Lainey Hitchman

Copyright © 2019 by Roy & Lainey Hitchman
Cover by: Lainey Hitchman
Editor: Roy Hitchman

All rights reserved. No part of this book may be reproduced in any form by any electronic or mechanical means including photocopying, recording, or information storage and retrieval without permission in writing from the authors.

ISBN: 978-1-911176-08-4
Book Website: www.hitchedtogether.com
Email: info@hitchedtogether.com

Give feedback on the book at:
feedback@hitchedtogether.com

Improving Communication

Roy & Lainey Hitchman

OTHER BOOKS IN THIS SERIES

Acknowledgements

Experience has taught us that a book never comes into being on its own. Each word, sentence, paragraph, page and chapter evolves from questions, conversations and a quest to learn more. A book therefore never has one exclusive creator. This book is the result of a great deal of research, many conversations and a lot of encouragement.

Thank you to those who shared their story with us, for those who spoke of their communication frustrations, and for those who cheered us on towards the goal of writing this book.

Preface

When we married, way back in 1989, Roy and I were unaware of the journey that God had in store for us. At that time, we were university students focused on forging ahead with married life and our future careers. During our journey, God caught our attention with the needs of couples and families in our local area. We realised that there was a lack of help for people struggling in their marriage, but also that there was very little for those who wanted to make sure that their relationships stayed healthy. God put on our hearts a call to minister to relationships. From this developed a ministry, teaching relationship workshops in churches around the UK and Europe. We had little idea, at that time, that God would eventually lead us to a mission field in Central Europe. Despite the geographical change we still have a very clear and defined call to minister to relationships.

Somewhere along that route, the realisation of the importance of communication developed. Maybe it grew from living in a country where connection, for us, was always in a non-native tongue. From this heightened awareness, we started to see how husbands and wives were trying to live in agreement, were communicating the same things but somehow the messages sent and received were miles apart. Whenever we saw this, or when we found ourselves operating as an interpreter for husbands and wives, we would make a mental note that a book addressing the area of communication in marriage was needed. This is that book! Long overdue, but nevertheless here in your hands.

Sometimes we think we understand because we know the meaning of the words we hear, or we have gotten to grips with the rules of grammar in a language. Without these elements, good communication wouldn't be possible, but these aspects are only a relatively small part of being able to communicate effectively. It's possible to assume that we understand each other's whole way of thinking, we forget that we might not share the same background and therefore don't have the same common view. As time moves on and as we become more familiar with each other, our individual cultures and our mannerisms, our communication with each other can and should improve.

Most couples would willingly admit that their communication could do with some improvement; although many people also point the finger of blame squarely at their spouse for communication failures. Whether you believe it's your fault, their fault or that you're both to blame, this book is for you! There is always room for improvement.

Communication can be classified anywhere on a broad scale from appalling all the way up to excellent. You may already have an idea of the quality of communication in your relationship. Where do you feel you are on that scale? Does your spouse agree? Wherever you are, you have picked up this book because you desire to improve, and that is a great place to start! Roy and I have been on the same journey, and have learned that communication takes practice and a lot of work. We are still in the process of growing in our skills, and we know it will take a lifetime to perfect them. That statement perhaps gives the impression that this is possible by human effort, but the reality is that we all need help. While good communication with family is desirable, good communication with God is essential if you are going to see the changes that you desire. As you embark on the journey of improving communication, we would encourage you to pray together and ask for His help. We simply cannot do it alone!

This book has been designed in bite-size sections with questions and tips so that you can easily chew over each one. The idea isn't to rush through the book but to give you the opportunity to pause and reflect, discuss the concepts and to give you practical principles that you can put into action.

Contents

Improving Communication 1
    Acknowledgements 5
    Preface 6

The Point of Communication 12
    What Do You Have in Common? 15
        The Desire to Belong 15
        The Desire for Friendship 19
        The Desire to Be Understood 21
        The Desire for Intimacy 24
        The Desire for Unity 26

The Problem with Communication 28
    What You Don't Have in Common 29
        The Same Brain 29
        The Same Gender 32
        The Same Goals 34
        The Same Communication Style 38

The Deterioration of Communication 41
    What went wrong? 42
        The Struggle to Be Real 44
        The Struggle to Acknowledge Responsibility 47
        The Struggle to Understand 50
        The Struggle to Hear 53

The Restoration of Communication 55
    What Happened to Change things? 56
        The Premise of Change 56
        The Process of Change 59
        The Pattern to Change 62

The Power to Change	66

The Power of Communication — 70
- When Your Tongue Needs Detoxing. — 72
  - The Difference between Constructive and Destructive Communication — 76
  - The Difference between Building Up and Tearing Down — 80
  - The Difference between Salty and Sour Conversations — 84

The Need to Learn Your Spouse's Language — 92
- What Rosetta Stone Can't Teach You — 94
  - The Language of the Heart — 97
  - Topical and Relational Communication — 99
  - The Comfort of the Mother Tongue — 102
  - The Funny Side of Life — 105

The Enigma Machine — 108
- How to Code Break — 111
  - Telepathic Delusions — 114
  - Advanced Level Charades — 117
  - Interpretations, Assumptions and Expectations — 120

The Components of Communication — 124
- Actions — 125
  - Actions Speak Louder Than Words — 127
  - The Motivation Behind Promises and Procrastination — 131
  - Body Language is Both Silent and Loud — 134
- Attitudes — 139
  - Is it a Mouth Problem or Heart Problem? — 139
  - Your Attitude is Determined by your Beliefs — 143
  - Your Beliefs can be Challenged and Your Attitude can Change — 147
  - It's Not What You Say but How You Say It — 152
  - It's Not What You Do But How You Do It — 156
- Words — 159
  - Words Decide Your Destination and Set Your Direction — 159
  - What to Say and What not to Say — 163
  - Pillow Talk — 167
  - You can't Nag and Whine your Way to a Better Marriage — 173

- Silence — 177
  - Learning to Shut Your Mouth — 177
  - When to Speak and When to be Quiet — 180
  - When to Say Nothing — 186
  - When to Say Something — 192
- Listening — 198
  - Listen with the Right Attitude — 201
  - Listen by Looking — 203
  - Listen Without Interrupting — 207

Bibliography — 215
Biography — 218

The Point of Communication

Lainey:
We were asked a challenging question when we went through our missionary training. The question was, 'What can you not live without?' We were not allowed to use standard answers such as God or the Bible. I quickly realised that one of my top ten was the ability to communicate. After hitting depression within the first few months of arrival on the mission field, I was in shock. At the time, I did not have a deep understanding of what I needed in order to break away from those feelings. Having a strong network of people who were willing to chat or send a note proved to be the difference between staying on the field or leaving early. Communication became an even higher priority for our family as a result. You may not be on a mission field, but we all have a 'mission' to develop healthy relationships; a mission that can only be achieved through healthy communication.

Communication is one of the most vital skills we need in life. It should be no surprise that it's equally essential within marriage. Good communication helps bridge gaps and build relationships. It is a tool which enables couples to share their hearts, their dreams, their visions and to come into agreement. On a more fundamental level, simply do life together.

We were designed to communicate; it is one of our most basic needs. When communication is lacking it brings separation, the feeling of loneliness, isolation and abandonment. Communication can lay a path to healing, restoration and renewed intimacy. Yet, communication is one of the areas in which couples find themselves most lacking and an area which appears to be most under attack. While this addresses the general reasons why communication is essential, let's get down to the nitty gritty of why you want to improve your communication with your spouse.

The 'Over to You!' section is designed to give you an opportunity to pause and think about how this applies to you. You can work through it alone or together with your spouse, questions are a great way to get conversations flowing! One word of caution though, if you're sharing your answers make sure that you don't use this as an opportunity to point the finger, that will disable conversation rather than helping it flow.

Over to You!

- Why did you decide to read this book?

- How would you describe your current communication with your spouse?

- What change would you like to see in your communication with your spouse?

- What outcome is most important to you?
    - Sharing dreams and aspirations
    - Being understood
    - Reaching agreement

- Do you have any other reasons for endeavouring to improve your communication skills?

#marriagetip

Look out for tips throughout the book, we've implemented them over the years and they've helped us improve our communication. We're confident they will help you too!

Set in place touch points in your weekly schedule so that you can spend quality time together, hang out, have fun and talk.

What Do You Have in Common?

Roy:
On the surface, when we first met, Lainey and I had little in common. Although we were both at university Lainey was studying English, and I was an engineering geek. Lainey was extroverted while I was introverted in nature. She was from Northern Ireland while I had spent most of my childhood in North Wales. However, through communication a connection was formed, we discovered things we had in common and soon after we had a sense that we belonged together.

The Desire to Belong

There has been a lot of research looking at the dynamics of successful relationships. One resounding conclusion is that as humans we have a fundamental need to belong and that communication is the primary tool to make this happen.

The Latin origin of the word communication is 'Communis' which points to having something in common. It's the same root that words like 'community' and 'commune' share. We could easily jump to the conclusion that to communicate effectively we need to have common interests. Of course, doing things together and having similar interests can be great but that is not what this implies. When we communicate, understanding is something we should have in common, yet even that does not quite cover it. 'Communis' doesn't just refer to interpreting the words that were spoken, it goes a lot deeper than that. Communication connects people, not only on the intellectual level but also on the emotional level. Good communication brings with it a sense of belonging.

The point of communication is to bring people together and give them a sense of affinity. This sense of belonging goes way beyond any physical attraction, it connects the soul. When a couple realises that they 'belong' together, it's because they have done a lot of communicating to get to that place, communication that hasn't been limited to topics or finding common interests but reaches further. They've shared hopes and dreams; they've shared thoughts and feelings, and they've felt understood. They have felt their spouse's empathy and know that their heart has been understood as well as their words.

For some couples that sense of belonging is missing. They aren't sure that they married the right person, and somehow haven't been able to feel that sense of unity. It's almost as though they operate within two different spheres and there is little or no overlap. Alternatively, you might have had that sense of belonging at the beginning of your relationship but have somehow lost that feeling along the way. If we continue with the 'sphere' analogy the points at which they overlap, or the touch points, have drifted apart until they no longer connect. If either of these examples sounds like your relationship, don't give up! You can regain that sense of belonging, or achieve it if you haven't ever felt that way.

Often that feeling of belonging has been expressed in the concept of 'soul mates' and the search for a marriage partner is often expressed by, 'I'm looking for the one'. Inadvertently, you can heap huge expectations on your spouse especially if you are holding on to the illusion that belonging is something that is easy and natural and doesn't require any work. In our book 'Adjusting Expectations'[1] we took a look at the Greek mythology that propagated the soul mates concept. It's easy to embrace the idea of two people perfectly fitting together when everyone has the same desire to belong. The problem is that when the one you thought was your soul mate does something that threatens your sense of belonging you could start to believe you didn't marry

---

1   978-1-911176-04-6 Adjusting Expectations Paperback

the right person. The illusion that each person has a soul mate is dangerous. Removing the 'soul mate' notion does not mean that you are doomed to never feel that sense of belonging. Rather, it frees you to realise that you can both grow and change to be the right one.

We're sure that over the years you have seen changes in yourself, differences in how you see things and how you do things. You'll also be aware of changes to how your relationship works and flows, how you feel about your spouse and how you interact with them. While you have been changing, your spouse has been changing too. Like all of us, there will be things that have changed for the better and things that have changed for the worse. Generally the older people become, the greater the tendency to be rigid in their thinking and their behaviour. Belonging requires us to remain pliable, to change together and to change with each other.

'BELONGING IS THE INNATE HUMAN DESIRE TO BE PART OF SOMETHING LARGER THAN US. BECAUSE THIS YEARNING IS SO PRIMAL, WE OFTEN TRY TO ACQUIRE IT BY FITTING IN AND BY SEEKING APPROVAL, WHICH ARE NOT ONLY HOLLOW SUBSTITUTES FOR BELONGING, BUT OFTEN BARRIERS TO IT. BECAUSE TRUE BELONGING ONLY HAPPENS WHEN WE PRESENT OUR AUTHENTIC, IMPERFECT SELVES TO THE WORLD, OUR SENSE OF BELONGING CAN NEVER BE GREATER THAN OUR LEVEL OF SELF-ACCEPTANCE'.
DR. BRENÉ BROWN
'THE GIFTS OF IMPERFECTION'

Cultivating the feeling of belonging is the responsibility of both husband and wife. This cultivation is not only achieved by having conversations, but it is attained by being willing to be vulnerable. The Bible describes this openness and unguardedness as being 'naked but not ashamed', it is only when you stop trying to 'cover up' your heart that you can truly be 'one' and feel that deep sense of what it is to be home.

Over to You!

- Do you feel like you belong together?
- If not, why not?
- What's contributing to that feeling?
- How do you connect with your spouse on both the intellectual (facts, figures, topics and situations) and emotional (feelings and empathy) level?
- On which of these two levels is it most difficult to connect with your spouse?

#marriagetip

Open a window into your life by sharing with your spouse how your day went (intellectual connection) and how you feel about the day (emotional connection).

The Desire for Friendship

Lainey:
When life started to get busy for the both of us, with Roy's career and with small children at home, our communication changed. Roy's focus was on his work day, and mine was on the exciting world of nappies (diapers), feeding schedules and the practicalities of parenting. It would be fair to say that in that season we saw our friendship suffer. Martin Luther's advice wasn't something we had in place.

> "LET THE WIFE MAKE THE HUSBAND GLAD TO COME HOME,
> AND LET HIM MAKE HER SORRY TO SEE HIM LEAVE".
> MARTIN LUTHER

In that season of our marriage, I felt at my loneliest. I had lost the connection with Roy that I once had and wasn't sure how to get it back. What I didn't realise back then was that I was longing for the friendship every married couple should enjoy. Unfortunately, because I felt starved of adult company, I shared the minute details of the day, which didn't inspire Roy. While Roy didn't mind hearing the headlines of how the day went and how I felt, he didn't want an inventory of how many nappies I had changed. Conversely, Roy would only share the headlines, which never fully satisfied my need to feel part of his life. It would lead to me asking further questions about the detail which was generally met with frustration. We both struggled to find common ground and subjects that interested us both. We had to work at adjusting our lives to accommodate our growing family and still make room for growing our friendship.

Friendship is a vital part of God's design for married life. Genesis tells us that it's not good for man to be alone and that is why God created marriage, yet many couples have fallen out of friendship. Where friendship is absent loneliness is present. Friendship is something that needs to be developed and nurtured which means it's essential to take a look at your communication patterns in your relationship.

Over to You!

- Do you speak to your spouse as you would a friend?
- How do you talk to your friends? What do you talk about?
- How do you talk to your spouse? What do you talk about?
- Has communication been reduced to giving each other instructions?
- Are you more pleasant to your work colleagues than to your spouse?
- Do you text each other with requests to run some errands on the way home or with messages of love?
- What are you doing to cultivate friendship with your spouse?

#marriagetip

When you speak to your spouse remind yourself that they are your friend. They aren't your slave, they aren't your child, and they aren't the enemy.

The Desire to Be Understood

Roy:
It was planning time again, one of those times where Lainey and I take a break from the usual, never-ending, procession of tasks with the purpose of getting on the same page. Lainey was talking, explaining something to me that would be happening. I felt I was following her points and I was able to recall past events and conversations about those events. We were communicating well. Everything was crystal clear - until it was not. The more Lainey talked, the more I realised I was in an entirely different book. My nods of encouragement and affirmation were slowly replaced by a confused expression as I realised I hadn't the slightest clue what Lainey was talking about. She was in full flow, excited, creative even, as she defined and described the things that would be happening in the near future.

For me, confusion gave way to panic as I realised I could no longer fake understanding and would have to interrupt her enthusiastic, path defining monologue. I desperately wanted to understand, I desired to communicate well, to work together to build our relationship but I felt that my mistranslation had potentially jeopardised that. It was challenging to admit I'd got it wrong and I ran the risk of upsetting Lainey by confessing I had no clue what she was talking about.

> 'Good communication is the bridge between confusion and clarity'.
> Nat Turner

Communication is only successful when someone receives the same intellectual and emotional message that the person speaking intended. In marriage, although many words are spoken, it is rare that a spouse receives and understands the message that was sent on both these relational levels. Both the intellectual and emotional levels are vital. It's crucial to achieve communication at the head level and the heart level. Of these two levels, heart to heart communication is generally the most difficult to achieve.

How often have you tried to bare your soul to your spouse only to be disappointed by their response? Maybe you have been met with a perplexed look, perhaps they have appeared disinterested, or they just don't understand what you are talking about. Your desire to be transparent and communicate clearly has backfired, and somehow you're left with a veil of confusion. You're not alone! Men and women certainly seem to transmit on two different wavelengths.

If you sometimes walk away from a conversation complaining that you 'simply don't get it', then it is very possible you aren't picking up on the language or cultural clues your spouse is sending. Deborah Tannen puts it like this, "An analogy is made between cross-cultural communication and a route on which someone has turned the signs around: the familiar signposts are there, but they don't lead in the right direction." Knowing this we could be tempted to give up trying, but we shouldn't draw the conclusion that trying to communicate is a lost cause. It's possible; it just takes a little effort and a lot of practice. Everyone has a different response to getting lost; some stubbornly keep on driving and refuse to ask the way, others get mad and blame his or her spouse for getting lost; the wise however stop and ask for directions. If you are wise, you will too!

1 Peter 3:7 throws down a challenge to husbands in particular. The verse says, "Likewise, husbands, live with your wives in an understanding way" (ESV) but what does understanding actually mean? There is a vast difference between knowing about someone and understanding them. This verse makes it a responsibility to get to grips with where your spouse is coming from. If we look at the original language the word 'understanding' in this verse more accurately means 'applied-knowledge', that's one step up from knowledge alone. It's

knowledge that has been acquired through study, so by implication; it's important to really get to know your spouse at a deeper level. Once you deeply know and understand them, you can work together to solve issues in your relationship. This type of understanding turns what you know into a very practical relationship tool. God's challenge to us all is to apply what we know, that's wisdom!

Over to You!

- *Do you feel your spouse understands you at the 'head' level?*
- *Do you feel understood at the 'heart' level?*
- *Do you generally come away from conversations feeling understood?*
- *Have you focused time and energy in trying to understand your spouse at a deeper level?*
- *Have you applied that knowledge to your relationship?*

#marriagetip

If you're getting lost in communication stop and ask for directions. If your spouse interrupts to ask for clarity, don't make them feel stupid for asking. You're both responsible for getting to a place of coherence and cohesion, clarity and unity.

The Desire for Intimacy

There are 'deep waters' within each one of us. Those things that are usually hidden from outside observers. Those deep thoughts and feelings should be safe to express in the safety of a marriage covenant without fear or concern. Intimacy in marriage is about much more than having sex; intimacy is about connecting body, soul and spirit and communication is a key to unlocking a deeper relationship.

> "Intimacy comes from "knowing" the other person at a deep level.
> If there are barriers to honesty,
> knowing is ruled out and the false takes over."
> Dr Henry Cloud (Boundaries in Marriage).

Communication is the pathway to emotional intimacy. It is the vehicle which leads you to a deeper relationship; however, it is important to realise that there is a difference in how the genders communicate. There is also a difference in what they talk about and what they view as an intimate conversation, so don't make the assumption that your spouse's needs are the same as yours.

If you are going to develop intimacy successfully at the emotional level, you will both need to learn to be transparent and vulnerable with each other. We've seen the biggest obstacle to having that level of openness is fear. Fear can be present for a number of reasons, perhaps you fear rejection if your spouse finds out what you truly think. You may fear judgement or fear your spouse's response. Usually, if someone is dealing with fear, they resort to secrecy.

> "Secrecy is the enemy of intimacy. Every healthy relationship is built
> on a foundation of honesty and trust".
> Dave Willis

Secrets are the lack of communication about certain things. They are the things that you don't want your spouse to know about. You might be keeping secrets about things you see as trivial or things which are pretty serious. They can range from keeping your spending habits quiet, to secrets about the past, about online activity, or about an affair. You need to realise that if you want to keep it secret (unless it's a surprise party or gift for your spouse) you are probably walking on dangerous ground. Don't sabotage your potential for intimacy with your spouse because you are unable to be honest.

Over to You!

- *Are you satisfied with the level of intimacy in your communication with your spouse?*
- *Are there any taboo subjects between you? Subjects you refuse to talk about?*
- *Are you keeping secrets from each other?*
- *If you are being cagey about your spouse looking at your computer or your phone what are you hiding? Why are you behaving in that way?*
- *Are you willing to work towards honesty and transparency?*

#marriagetip

If you want your spouse to be more transparent and vulnerable make sure you are safe to share with. Manage your reactions to what they share and don't break their confidence by telling others what was only meant for your ears.

The Desire for Unity

Many things can give you insight into the condition of your relationship, but few are as poignant as the use of 'single' vocabulary. Me, mine, I and my, are four innocent words, or so they would seem. They are certainly harmless if the person using that vocabulary is a single person; however, if you are married, it could be a warning sign that something is amiss with your relationship. That's not saying there is never a time to use these words in marriage, but they can be indicative of a 'single' mindset at best and a narcissistic one at worst.

> Unity is oneness of purpose, Not sameness of persons.
> Tony Evans

When you get married, there should be a transition in your thinking. Those who come from extremely independent cultures can find this extraordinarily difficult, and their lives as a married couple could be classified as 'married single' rather than married. Your mindset and thought processes influence the vocabulary you use. It's important to remember that you aren't sailing through life alone, making decisions on your own, and you are not in a part-time marriage. You are married full-time, and you need to move from being single in your mindset, behaviour and speech to becoming what the Bible calls one-flesh. That transition in communication makes it clear that you are in this together.

> For this reason, a man will leave his father and mother
> and be united to his wife, and the two will become one flesh.'
> So they are no longer two, but one flesh.
> Therefore what God has joined together, let no one separate."
> **Mark 10:7-9 NIV**

These verses outline a process of transition and a priority shift which is essential to grasp. The priority doesn't move from parents and family to self but to a new 'self' called 'one-flesh', your marriage relationship. It's a relationship which demands you give up any residue of selfishness and prioritise your marriage relationship.

Unfortunately, narcissism is on the rise, and even if a full-blown narcissistic disorder isn't something you have to deal with, there is evidence that an over-inflated view of self and indifference to others is on the rise. That's why the 'me, myself and I' words can be a warning sign that you need to pause and think about your spouse and what their needs are.

Over to You!

- *When your spouse expresses a need do you take note or dismiss it?*
- *When your spouse expresses his/her need, do you listen or combat it with one of your own?*
- *What do you talk about?*
  - *Do you focus on your own favourite topics and check out when your spouse starts to talk about what interests them?*
  - *Do you feel your spouse does that to you?*
- *Do you have a tendency to monologue instead of having a dialogue with your spouse?*

#marriagetip

Unity isn't having everyone agree with you, nor is it focused on having your needs met. Unity is achieved when both spouses lay down selfishness and focus on each other.

The Problem with Communication

What You Don't Have in Common

The Same Brain

Lainey:
If communication is something that is designed to bring people together, to develop a sense of unity and a sense of intimacy, why is it so difficult? Roy and I often approach communication from entirely different angles. Part of the reason why we approach topics differently is that we don't share the same brain. Our past, our experiences, our personalities and of course the fact that Roy is male and I am female account for the differences in our perspectives and some of the problems we have in communication.

While we usually steer clear of pigeonholing people, in this section, we will be guilty of making generalisations and stereotypes as we approach the subject of gender in the context of language. Of course, we recognise that there are exceptions and broad brushstrokes in no way portray everyone. It is true to say though that the differences in communication styles represented by a husband and wife will also complicate an already complex issue.

The Christian comedian Mark Gungor in his seminar "Laugh Yourself to a Better Marriage" has a session called "The Tale of Two Brains". In it he jokes about how men and women are wired differently. He goes on to explain that the two sexes think about, prioritise and compartmentalise issues in such a diverse way that there is plenty of room for confusion. Gungor's audiences tend to fall into fits of laughter because they can relate to his humorous take on real-life issues. You may be like me and need a bit more evidence to back this idea up, and the evidence is undoubtedly available! 'Male brains utilise nearly seven times more grey matter for activity while female brains use almost ten times more white matter.'²

So how does this fact influence communication? Well, let's say that Roy is working and using his grey matter to focus on what he is doing. He gets a bit lost in that grey matter because it's a localised part of the brain. Roy's tunnel vision when it comes to projects means that I find it difficult to catch his attention. When I do break through, I don't always get a sweet reply because he's been designed to focus, and that sometimes means being insensitive to what's going on around him. Your spouse might do the same thing when they're watching TV, fixing something or watching football.

Roy has his own challenges when approaching me in 'white matter' mode. I kick into full multi-tasking mode, and Roy can sometimes feel that I'm not focused on him or what he's saying. Even if I repeat what he has just said it can still come across as though I'm parroting what he said without it sinking in. If I'm honest, then I'll admit that often that is precisely the case. Multi-tasking might get many jobs done at the one time, but it isn't helpful in the context of building a connection.

If confusion comes into play, it can lead to someone being hurt, and being wounded can cause someone to erect protective barriers around them which then leads to broken communication. You can hopefully see the potential downward spiral; it would be smart, therefore, to learn how to make sense of some of the confusion. Of course, the ability to intensely focus on one thing or multi-task isn't the only difference in how people think. We are all individuals with our life experiences, our own perspectives our individual priorities and takes on life. Even though, over years of married life, couples tend to become more like one another they will never share the same brain. God made <u>every one of us u</u>nique!

2   Gregory L. Jantz Ph.D. Hope for Relationships

In the same way that twins don't share the same fingerprints, no-one has the same thought patterns. Even though our brains might be wired differently, it doesn't mean that it's an impossible task to agree: to be of one mind. If we get on the same wavelength as the Holy Spirit, it's possible to achieve a whole new level of communication.

So if there is any encouragement in Christ, any comfort from love, any participation in the Spirit, any affection and sympathy, complete my joy by being of the same mind, having the same love, being in full accord and of one mind. Do nothing from selfish ambition or conceit, but in humility count others more significant than yourselves. Let each of you look not only to his own interests, but also to the interests of others. Have this mind among yourselves, which is yours in Christ Jesus.
Philippians 2:1-5 ESV

Over to You!

- *Do you fit the stereotype or do you differ in some way?*
- *Can you identify any areas in which you think differently to your spouse?*
    - *Priorities*
    - *Like and dislikes*
    - *Opinions (from how household tasks should be done through to politics)*
- *How can you change your approach to your spouse now that you understand more about your differences?*

#marriagetip

You don't have to share the same opinions to have a successful marriage. You do need to respect each other's views and recognise that your spouse has the right to a different perspective.

The Same Gender

Many years ago Roy and I became aware of the differences in how genders communicate while we were at a seminar. The speaker said, 'Women often use the telephone as a bonding tool while men use it to communicate information.' It certainly was a stereotype that summarised our situation well, but it only touches the tip of the iceberg of gender differences in communication.

The most significant difference between men and women and their style of communication boils down to the fact that men and women view the purpose of conversations differently[3]. Men often consider conversations as a tool through which to get information or give information; they use communication to achieve a tangible goal. Women also have a goal in mind but it is less visible, and therefore men struggle to see the objective.

There is nothing more frustrating for a wife than a husband who communicates in headlines only. She wants to hear the details of the day, what happened, who said what, she wants the full newspaper article and is not going to be satisfied with the caption.

Women need to communicate deeply in order to build intimacy in a relationship and getting an answer which is only a few words long builds a wall rather than intimacy. Unwittingly husbands can often give their wives the impression that they don't want their wives involved in their lives and exude an unintentional 'mind your own business' attitude.

For a man, it can be very frustrating when his wife won't just let him relax when he gets home from work. He has said all that he wants to say, the day was 'fine', why the need for all the detail? Roy

---

[3] Merchant, 2012

is definitely a headline man; it's how he compartmentalises work and home life. Asking him questions about his day can snap him back to the stresses of the workplace, but that doesn't mean that partners are doomed to be frustrated for the rest of their lives.

You can't share the same gender, but you can learn to appreciate the differences and work towards something that you are both happy with. Different is just different; it's not wrong, and it's healthier to recognise the strengths that both of you have instead of searching for the weaknesses. Roy and I discovered that when we each understood what we needed from conversations, it helped us appreciate each other more and be more willing to meet in the middle.

Over to You!

- What is your biggest frustration regarding how your spouse communicates?
- Do you know what frustrates them with how you communicate?
- Can you relate to the stereotype or is your experience different?

#marriagetip

Consider each other's needs in conversation and make an effort to step out of your comfort zone to communicate in a way which will reach their heart.

The Same Goals

Again, at the risk of bowing to stereotypes men and women tend to have different goals when they converse. If you don't share the same goals, it's essential to get to grips with what they are. If you're struggling to answer that question, it usually helps to look at what each sex generally talks about with the same sex in their own culture.

- What do men generally talk about when they are with friends?

- What do women share with each other when they meet?

- What does this tell you about what each gender is looking for in conversation?

One typical complaint women have is that their spouses are always trying to fix things. If you take a look at how men use conversation, then you'll start to understand why that is the case. When men chat about things, there is usually a purpose in mind.

I've often observed Roy talking to his friend Peter. Between the two of them they systematically work through the problems they see in the world and solve them. They take a logical approach and rarely express how they feel about those things, in a sense the emotion behind it is revealed by their passion for particular topics rather than because they use their words to express their emotions. Studies show that men are viewed as more likely than women to offer solutions to problems in order to avoid further, seemingly unnecessary, discussions of interpersonal problems[4].

When Roy is talking to Peter, I'm usually in an in-depth conversation

---

4   (Baslow & Rubenfield, 2003)

with Kati (Peter's wife). We also talk about a lot of things, but we are not so focused on solving problems as talking about our lives, our families and our feelings. Just offloading the cares and concerns of the day is enough to make us feel better even if a solution is not in sight.

The other day Roy and I both felt frustrated after having a conversation about my health. I had been given the bad news by my doctor that I needed to restrict my diet further. I felt pretty down about it and wanted to talk about it, well perhaps it's more accurate to say I wanted a little sympathy. Roy wanted to swiftly and efficiently get to the root of the problem and sort it, he wanted to know what food we needed to buy and what we needed to cook differently. I found my irritation level rising the more we talked, I merely wanted him to acknowledge my feelings. Roy was searching for solutions and I was searching for intimacy, a sense of closeness; the feeling of being understood. Roy cared deeply about what was happening, but his expression of caring came through doing something practical.

Even when you know the theory, it's sometimes difficult to remember to put it into practice. We're getting better at it, but we are still in the process of change.

> "MEN MOST OFTEN KNOW WHAT THEY WANT,
> YET THEY ARE NOT ALWAYS SURE HOW THEY FEEL.
> WOMEN MOST OFTEN KNOW HOW THEY FEEL,
> YET THEY MAY NOT ALWAYS KNOW WHAT THEY WANT."
> KEN POIROT

One mistake that we see many couples making is that they expect their spouse to meet all of their emotional needs, they expect their friendship with their spouse to closely resemble that of other friendships. I undoubtedly can say that Roy is my best friend, but he would be bored to tears if I talked to him about some of the things I talk about with my friendship group. Likewise, when Roy dives deep into solving the social and political problems of the world with his male friends he explores topics that we rarely talk about. When Roy launches into the technical or engineering world, I'm equally at a loss.

It's valid to ask, in the light of that revelation, how and why we consider ourselves to still be best friends. Well, the differentiation lies in this: Roy knows my strengths, my failings, my emotions (whether they are good, bad or ugly), he takes the time to listen to my heart, and he knows things about me that no one else knows. I trust Roy implicitly, I know I can trust him enough to be fully open and honest with him. I also get the privilege to hear Roy's heart, to understand his private thoughts to listen to the things that he doesn't talk about with the guys, things that he feels are only safe to share in our relationship.

Deborah Tannen, a sociolinguist, put forward the view that men seek independence and women seek intimacy, the goals of men and women being diametrically opposite. It certainly seems true in other areas of society but is this the same in marriage? We believe she is partially right and partially wrong, let us explain. In our first book, Bringing Worlds Together,[5] we talked about a power struggle that was established between husbands and wives as a result of the fall. Adam and Eve's sin had consequences. The desire to rule over one another and dominate each other was the unfortunate result. It's a tendency that needs to be fought against not in the sense of resisting each other, but in prayer.

So, on the one hand, there is a fight for independence, but on the other hand, it isn't reflective of what we see and hear from couples. In the majority of cases both husbands and wives long for intimacy and closeness, it isn't only a female desire. The problem comes when one or both resort to control to try and achieve that intimacy. If you both ask God to help you learn to love one another in a self-sacrificial way and let go of your own agenda, you'll start to see a change in your

[5] Bringing Worlds Together ISBN: 978-1-911176-022

communication.

Over to You!

- Do you struggle to express what you want?
- Do you find it difficult to talk about feelings?
- Do you recognise what your own goals are in communication?
- Have you understood what your spouse needs when you have conversations?
- Rather than expecting your spouse to make all the changes, is there something you can do differently in this area?

#marriagetip

Since you don't have the same goals in communication, try playing by your spouse's rules. If they need you to get to the point quickly so they can understand what they need to do, try shortcutting some of the detail. If they require you to listen to their thought process, then try not to hurry them along. If you both respect each other's communication 'routes', you'll find your conversations have better results.

The Same Communication Style

My second language is sign language, it's a beautiful language which is incredibly expressive. It's also a language, like any other, that allows your personality to shine through. When I was learning to sign I was told that everyone has a signing box, a space in which they sign. For some that box is huge, they are the equivalent of the loud people in the room who draw attention because of their volume. There are those who have a tiny signing box, or signing space and they are the whisperers who are more comfortable in a less overt form of expression.

If you've ever been in a room with your spouse and they turn to you and ask you to keep the volume down, it's probably because they would rather curl up in a ball and hide than have attention drawn to them through loud conversation. When our son was younger, we used to joke that he came without a remote control and the volume was stuck on loud, even his whispers were loud. Thankfully as Ryan got older, he learned to communicate at a more comfortable volume for his listeners than when he was tiny.

Being aware of your own communication style and how it affects others, especially your spouse, is essential. If you find that your spouse is continually digging you in the ribs because you're talking too much and not leaving room for others in the conversation, it's worth taking note. If you're sharing what you consider to be a funny story but your spouse finds it humiliating, reign in your humour and respect their wishes.

Conversely, it's not uncommon to find someone who struggles because they feel they need to carry the conversation for their spouse in public. Someone who is quiet may find it difficult to understand how their behaviour can come across as rude, but in certain cultures where small talk is expected it can. Some hide behind the title of 'introvert' to excuse their silence in public settings just as someone who is loud might hide behind the label 'extrovert'.

The big question is, does something need to change because your spouse would like it to or should they simply accept you as you are? To answer that question we need to understand the difference between personality and character. There are also traits normally associated with each of these personality types, but they are perhaps best summarised in terms of gaining or expending energy during social interactions. Extroverts are more outgoing, and introverts tend to be happier in a small group or in their own company. If someone is an extrovert, at the core of their being, that is not likely to change. Nor is it possible for an introvert to decide to change their personality. However, some character issues can be addressed.

If an extrovert draws energy from being with people, that does not excuse them demanding all the attention and ignoring another's needs. In fact, that behaviour is more in line with narcissistic traits. An introvert might feel drained by being with people but it doesn't mean they can't be polite, greet people and have a pleasant conversation. If there is a fear of social interaction, then there is a deeper issue that needs to be ministered to. Being introverted or extroverted refers to personality, but being egocentric or, at the other end of the scale, desiring to be invisible, points to an area of character that needs work.

Over to You!

- *Communication style can include the volume at which you speak, how much you talk, and what you talk about. Are there any areas you need to work on?*
- *Are you both comfortable with the volume your spouse speaks at?*

- *Do either of you talk too much or too little in the other's opinion?*
- *Do either of you broach subjects which you are uncomfortable talking about in public conversation?*
- *Do either of you feel embarrassed or humiliated by your spouse when you are in company?*

#marriagetip

Be considerate of each other's needs in your home and in public. If you know you've embarrassed or humiliated your spouse, then ask for their forgiveness. If you recognise that you have areas which need 'work', then try and find someone who can help you learn the skills you need.

The Deterioration of Communication

What Went Wrong?

> "No matter what job you have in life,
> your success will be determined
> 5% by your academic credentials,
> 15% by your professional experiences,
> and 80% by your communication skills".
> Stephen Wang

If this is true of our ability to be successful in a work situation, then is it possible that you are underestimating the role of communication in your relationship?

We've met many people who are great communicators in the workplace. They are able to articulate their ideas and express themselves coherently in a work setting, but something breaks down when they are at home. Maybe that's been your experience too. Have you ever wondered why?

It seems sensible to ask the obvious question. What went wrong with communication? Why do so many couples struggle with the fundamentals of sharing experiences and emotions with one another? Right from the beginning of the Bible, we see communication in operation. God communicated His wishes and desires for mankind at creation.

> **Then the LORD God said, "It is not good that the man should be alone; I will make him a helper fit for him."**
> **Genesis 2:18 ESV**

God created us to interact, to do life together, to communicate. He modelled communication in the garden of Eden. Genesis 3:8 implies that he had a regular habit of conversation with Adam and Eve.

He didn't restrict the role of husbands and wives to being helpful or working together, but He met man's inbuilt need for companionship, communication and community. God's design was not that two people should get married and feel alone, His model was that two people would get married and know that they belong together.

Over to You!

- *Do you feel lonely in your marriage?*
- *Do you make it a habit to have regular conversations?*
- *Do you spend time together talking to God about what's going on in your lives?*

#marriagetip

Set aside a minimum of 15 device free minutes every day and talk to each other. Also, establish a regular time each day to pray together and read the Bible.

The Struggle to Be Real

In Genesis, we see a model of marriage which was naked. In Genesis 2:25 we are told that Adam and Eve were naked yet felt no shame. I'm pretty sure that this wasn't just about body image, but something else was going on here. It takes digging below the surface to find out what it means at a deeper level.

The word 'shame' is the word 'בוש'(bosh) in Hebrew. It's translated in other parts of the Bible not only as the state of being ashamed but also that of being confounded or confused. Many couples don't struggle to be naked physically in front of each other but do find it difficult to be emotionally and spiritually open. We have been made in three parts: body, soul and spirit. In the physical sense; being naked should be without shame, in the emotional sense; without fear of being misunderstood or misunderstanding, and in the spiritual sense; with transparency, because there is nothing to hide.

Unfortunately, sin brought along with it the desire to hide from each other. Before the fall being naked didn't result in shame, confusion or being confounded, after the fall Adam and Eve were rummaging for anything to cover themselves up. Blame entered the scene, and you can sense the frustration in the relationship between Adam and Eve.

Our struggles today aren't dissimilar. People struggle to be 'real' and open with each other. Couples often don't fully disclose their emotions, or if they do, it's in an unhealthy way. This isn't something which impacts the soul solely, spiritually husbands and wives also might not be open about what they are facing and what they are struggling with.

In their book 'Why Women Talk and Men Walk', Patricia Love and

Steven Stosny explain that often the blame for failed relationships is placed squarely on poor communication, but the issue is much deeper than that. Emotions are lying under the surface that skew communication attempts. One is fear, and the other is shame. You can see this come into play in the Genesis account but how does it work in marriage?

Just as Adam and Eve rummaged about to find something to cover their bodies, couples often search for something to hide behind. If one spouse feels confronted they quickly pour out the reasons why they acted as they did or said what they said. This is in an attempt to justify their behaviour and avoid disapproval from their spouse. Another strategy is resisting getting pulled into conversations which have the potential to go in the wrong direction. This is often a default, especially for men. Have you ever tried to discuss your relationship and felt it didn't result in fixing things but just in making you feel terrible? That's shame kicking into gear. The underlying emotions make it difficult to talk about something purely on the logical level.

When a husband or wife puts into play resistance tactics and refuses to talk about an issue, it often triggers fear in their spouse. No one can mind read, so it's incredibly frustrating and provides a lot of 'empty space' to fill. Fear floods into that empty space, fear of rejection, fear of abandonment, fear that the relationship is broken. Fear and shame are in the same family, and they're good at playing tag.

Over to You!

- *Do you struggle to be real with your spouse?*
- *Can you identify areas which you are reluctant to share because of shame?*
  - *Do you know of any topics that are off limits for your spouse?*

- What's your default avoidance tactic if you're uncomfortable with a conversation?
  - How does your spouse avoid tricky subjects?
- Can you identify any fear regarding the stability of your relationship if you were to be vulnerable with each other?
- Do you actively create a safe environment in which your spouse feels safe to share?

#marriagetip

When you sense negative emotions coming up in you, don't place the blame for those feelings on your spouse. Instead, take time to consider why those emotions are there. How long have you felt that way? Have you always had that response to conflict? If you discover that you're dealing with shame or fear, ask God to help you process those emotions and to set you free from their hold.

The Struggle to Acknowledge Responsibility

Shame's sibling is blame, and the blame game came into play immediately after the fall when God challenged Adam and Eve regarding what happened. Their relationship with God had already shifted because they felt guilty for their actions and it was from that position of guilt that they answered the questions God asks.

> **And he said, "Who told you that you were naked? Have you eaten from the tree that I commanded you not to eat from?"The man said, "The woman you put here with me—she gave me some fruit from the tree, and I ate it." Then the Lord God said to the woman, "What is this you have done?"The woman said, "The serpent deceived me, and I ate."**
> **Genesis 3:11-13 NIV**

Adam's response is interesting. He blames God since He gave him the woman and he blames the woman because she gave him the fruit. You can almost hear him brushing off responsibility, after all, he just ate what was handed to him by the woman God had given to him. Yet, Adam knew God's command first hand, and he should have taken a stand not only for himself but for his wife. His excuses fall flat because his acknowledgement that he ate the fruit is overshadowed by blaming others for his own behaviour.

Eve's response is very much 'the devil made me do it'. She doesn't blame Adam or God; she blames the serpent and at the same time minimises her intelligence. God had created Eve as an intelligent woman who was made to have dominion over the earth.

> Then God said, "Let us make mankind in our image, in our likeness, so that they may rule over the fish in the sea and the birds in the sky, over the livestock and all the wild animals, and over all the creatures that move along the ground."
> Genesis 1:26 NIV

We've seen people 'dumb themselves down' and assume a position of weakness or ignorance as a technique to deflect responsibility. It could be argued that both Adam and Eve were just telling it how it was but what they don't do is own up to their personal responsibility for their decisions.

We've talked in one of our other books[6] about fundamental attribution error but here is a quick summary of how blame works in marriage. One of the spouses has an annoying tendency to maximise the effect of their husband or wife's words or actions on their own emotions. In other words, it's their spouses fault for what they say, what they do and what they feel. If plans are messed up, it's their spouse's fault if they don't feel good about life. Their spouse effectively becomes a scapegoat. They do all of this while simultaneously ignoring or minimising the effects of their own actions on the wellbeing of their spouse. Somehow, anything that goes wrong is attributed to the action or inaction of their partner while anything that proves successful was their idea.

These patterns are repeated all too often. The result is either the partner starts believing that they are the source of all that is wrong in the marriage, or, they react against the propaganda resulting in sparks, or a sulky and resistant spouse.

---

[6] Adjusting Expections ISBN: 9781911176053

Over to You!

- Do you struggle to take responsibility for your words, attitudes and actions?
- What/Who do you tend to blame?
  - *Your childhood?*
  - *Your spouse or kids?*
  - *God?*

#marriagetip

Next time you find yourself blaming your spouse, pause and consider your words, behaviour and tone of voice. Is there anything you said or did that escalated the argument? Is there anything you could have done differently?

The Struggle to Understand

Genesis 11 adds further clarity to the difficulties we have today with communication. It's a story of ambition which becomes a tale of confusion. The story of Babel is of a united people who shared a single language and a single goal, a goal to make a name for themselves. The goal, however, was not in agreement with God's plan for them. The Bible relates the story of how one language became many, of how coherence became confusion, as God set out to confound them.

> **Go to, let us go down, and there confound their language, that they may not understand one another's speech.**
> **Genesis 11:7 KJV**

The word confound is the word 'balal' in Hebrew which many attribute to being the origin of the name Babel. It means to confuse, they were doomed to misunderstand one another. While there are obvious difficulties with multiple languages, the same issues seem to translate into married life. Intercultural couples might find it challenging to learn each other's languages to the degree where they fully understand each other. At least these couples know that there is much room for confusion because they aren't speaking in their native tongue. Those couples who have the blessing of sharing the same mother tongue often don't realise that they still need to put the work in to understand their spouse.

There are evidently two sides to the confusion problem. Often we don't just struggle to understand, but we struggle to be understood. Indirectness regularly contributes to this problem.

Your spouse is not being sneaky when they ask you to do something in an indirect way. They are most likely not trying to deliberately trap you or trip you up! They have grown up in a home in which those indirect requests are recognised and understood without explanation.

We've already established that only a tiny proportion of meaning is communicated by words. I don't have any idea the percentage of communication that is taken up with indirectness, but I do know that indirectness includes hints, assumptions and a lot of cultural background knowledge.

The "Would you like to...?" question is one such example for Roy and I. In my family background it is an indirect request for something to be done which means something very different than its surface meaning. In fact, to me it means "Please do it now". In Roy's childhood home 'Would you like to...?' meant just that and a yes or no answer could be given without causing offence.

Some will respond to this story by wondering why I didn't just say what I meant, why didn't I simply blurt out my request. Why go to the trouble of playing games when I could communicate clearly? The problem is that from my cultural standpoint I had been clear. I had no idea that there was any room for confusion. I had no intention of hinting or of being indirect.

There have been many cross-cultural studies done regarding the confusion which arises in business. Deals have been struck only to result in disappointment where one or both parties came away scratching their heads wondering what went wrong. Blame is usually the first defence people grab hold of. Integrity is questioned, and mistrust is birthed. If that happens in business, we can assume that it also occurs in marriage.

Indirect communication is like a giant invisible spoon which stirs up conflict. Can the problem of indirect communication be solved? Unfortunately, there isn't a way of removing the spoon; indirect communication is here to stay like it or not. There is a way however of making that 'spoon' more visible and preventing it from stirring things up in your relationship.

Over to You!

- Identify the spoon or spoons. If there are requests you are making that are ignored, then you need to find out if the request was understood.

- Are there any words you both use but understand differently? If you find yourselves arguing over semantics, it's possible that you attribute a different meaning to those words. Understanding your spouse's definition will improve your communication.

#marriagetip

Learn to be more direct. I have had to embrace the fact that if I ask more directly, Roy will respond. I still feel that I am being somewhat impolite, but I know that it is worth avoiding conflict by being more obvious. Also, learn to translate the indirectness correctly. On occasions when I have forgotten to be direct and revert to my "Would you like to…?" requests Roy usually laughs and translates it for me. "Did you mean…?"

The Struggle to Hear

Another detail which can sometimes be missed by a quick read of the story is that the Hebrew word 'understand' is translated in other parts of the Bible as listen, or hear. In the area of communication, listening is as vital as speaking. It's a skill that needs to be learned and developed as much as the gift of speaking with clarity. Couples often do a lot of talking, but they don't do a lot of listening. Without actively listening it's impossible to understand what your spouse is trying to communicate.

There is a big difference between hearing and listening, and that contrast can make a significant impact on your relationship. The primary differentiation is the purpose for which you want the information. It has been said that "Hearing is the gaining of information for oneself, while listening is caring for and being empathetic toward others." In marriage especially we need to become good listeners.

Some spouses 'hear' because they want to gather evidence against their spouse, or support their own argument. Listening gets beyond the selfish and searches not only for superficial meaning but hears the heart. It takes time to learn to listen in this new way. Rather than analysing the words, and understanding solely at the cognitive level, you gain a deeper understanding, one that reaches the emotional level.

Listening isn't a passive state which requires no response. It's an active, intentional engagement that conveys you care enough to be quiet and hear another's heart.

Over to You!

- *How good are you at listening? Does your spouse agree?*
- *Which do you struggle with the most?*
  - *Being Real*
  - *Acknowledging Responsibility*
  - *Understanding and being understood*
  - *Actively listening?*

#marriagetip

Allow your spouse to finish their sentence before you respond. When you respond try asking a question to clarify or try reflecting back what they said to check your interpretation.

The Restoration of Communication

What Happened to Change things?

The Premise of Change

It's clear why communication deteriorated and became the mess that it is today, but that doesn't mean it has to stay that way. Just as God communicated His plans for mankind clearly at creation, He has continued to communicate with us. The gospel is the ultimate communication of the 'good news' we needed to hear.

> **And the Word became flesh and dwelt among us,
> and we have seen his glory,
> glory as of the only Son from the Father,
> full of grace and truth.
> John 1:14 ESV**

It's incredible that when your words aren't enough and you struggle to express yourself, that you can entirely rely on the one who is called the 'Word' to help you communicate love to your spouse. You can follow Jesus example and what the Bible has to say about how to relate to each other to help you have healthy communication.

If you want to see true change in your life and in your marriage and in your communication, then you need to understand the spiritual side of things. Since we are a three-part being, we can't ignore the spiritual element of who we are. In fact, it's possible that self-confidence in your own communication abilities can actually derail your relationship. Often the way we think we should approach an issue is contrary to the way that God suggests we deal with things.

> For my thoughts are not your thoughts,
> neither are your ways my ways, declares the LORD.
> For as the heavens are higher than the earth, so are my ways
> higher than your ways and my thoughts than your thoughts.
> Isaiah 55:8-9 ESV

We were created as a three-part being, body, soul and spirit. The Bible makes it clear that because of sin we need to go through a regeneration process. Renewal is a spiritual work, and Jesus made that possible through His ultimate sacrifice and became our rescuer.

> For He delivered us from the domain of darkness
> and transferred us to the kingdom of His beloved Son, in whom
> we have redemption, the forgiveness of sins.
> Colossians 1:13-14 ESV

This wasn't just a physical rescue, but it was a spiritual one also. In fact, the spiritual rescue is the immediate completed work.

> Jesus replied, "Very truly I tell you, no one can
> see the kingdom of God unless they are born again."
> "How can someone be born when they are old?"
> Nicodemus asked. "Surely they cannot enter a second time
> into their mother's womb to be born!" Jesus answered,
> "Very truly I tell you, no one can enter the kingdom of God unless they are born of water and the Spirit. Flesh gives birth to flesh, but the Spirit gives birth to spirit. You should not be surprised at my saying, 'You must be born again.'
> John 3:3-7 NIV

When you are born again, when God transforms your spirit then you can start your journey to personal transformation and towards enjoying a marriage that is transformed. Instead of responding from our humanness we have the potential to tap into God's wisdom and understanding. He gives us His written word and His Holy Spirit to help and guide us in all areas of life including how we do relationships. The change you want to see in your marriage is possible with God's help.

Over to You!

- *Have you recognised your need for God's help in your relationship?*
- *Do you pray for your spouse and for the communication between you to improve?*
- *When you respond to your spouse do you react from your humanness or do you respond with God's heart for them?*

#marriagetip

If you have already made a commitment to follow Christ but haven't seen the change in your relationship yet then ask Him to help you to learn and grow in this area. If you first listen to God, He will enable you to listen to your spouse.

The Process of Change

We've already said there isn't a magic pill to improve communication; it takes hard work. The problem is though, that when people try to implement change, they often do it without taking into consideration their design. Let's break that down a little. We've just examined the most fundamental change anyone can make, and that is being awakened spiritually, but we also have a soul and a spirit. Most people try and tackle communication on the soulish level. The soul can be defined as your mind, your will and your emotions.

- The mind - your knowledge, your intellect, your thoughts.

- The will - the choices you make and the desires you have.

- The emotions - the feelings you have including those you choose not to express.

People often try and change the body by working the body harder, and they try and change the soul through soulish means, using their mind, will and emotions to solve their problems.

This is how it plays out in practice if a couple uses soulish communication. A problem comes up between a husband and wife, and they try and sort it out using their mind. They both use their brains to work out a better argument, a way to convince the other that their opinion is the best. Some aren't as skilful with the tongue, so they add weight to their convictions by using their will. This type of personality will deliberately go against something their spouse wants to do, and instead, they do the opposite. They make their own choices regardless of the impact on the one they profess to love and often resort to passive aggressive or stubborn behaviour. Others use their emotions to manipulate their spouse through tears or tantrums, whichever is more effective in ensuring that they get their own way.

All of this is a far cry from the pattern that God has laid out for us. He wants us to move from soulish communication to spiritual communication. Galatians 5:13-26 holds many keys to transformation and what living life by the Spirit should be like. It's worthwhile diving in deeply to understand these principles rather than just skipping over them.

> **You, my brothers and sisters, were called to be free.**
> **But do not use your freedom to indulge the flesh;**
> **rather, serve one another humbly in love.**
> **Galatians 5:13 NIV**

We're free but that doesn't mean that we are free to do what we want or to be selfish, we can be free from selfishness so we can serve one another humbly in love. The spirit transforms the soul (the mind, the will and the emotions) and when we follow God's will instead of our will it has an impact on our actions. The Bible often uses the expression 'the flesh' to highlight our soulish or human responses to situations.

> **For you are still of the flesh.**
> **For while there is jealousy and strife among you,**
> **are you not of the flesh and behaving only in a human way?**
> **1 Corinthians 3:3 ESV**

Over to You!

Think back to arguments that you've had with your spouse, which of the following areas have you had the most trouble with?

- *The mind.*
  - *Struggling to understand something from your spouse's point of view because it cuts across what you view as an intellectual or logical argument.*
  - *Struggling not to think negatively about your spouse when they oppose your opinion or decisions.*
  - *Struggling with something else you're thinking about?*
- *The will.*
  - *Struggling to make decisions which are best for everyone not just best for you.*
  - *Struggling to do something you know is your responsibility, but you find it difficult to follow through.*
  - *Struggling with some other issue to do with your will?*
- *The emotions.*
  - *Struggling to keep your temper in check and not lose your temper with your spouse.*
  - *Struggling to keep it together rather than breaking down in tears.*
  - *Struggling with something else emotionally?*

We've deliberately used the word 'struggling' repeatedly through these questions. Change is not just a one-time decision, change is a daily choice to wrestle with your mind, your will and your emotions and make them subject to God's mind, His will and His heart for others.

#marriagetip

It can be difficult to break negative patterns of thinking, negative choices or deal with difficult emotions. When you are struggling to change, remember that you can bring those things to God and ask for His help. Focus on what you can change (you) rather than what you can't change.

The Pattern to Change

We've talked a lot about change, but it's worth remembering that it's too easy to impose one's own idea about what communication should look like in marriage. God has a pattern and a plan for your communication which will surpass yours. So what is God's blueprint for change? Galatians not only reveals more of God's plan but gives us a strategy regarding how you can achieve it.

> **For the whole law is fulfilled in one word:**
> **"You shall love your neighbour as yourself."**
> **But if you bite and devour one another,**
> **watch out that you are not consumed by one another.**
> **Galatians 5:14-15 ESV**

Do you ever get hung up on the details, and miss the big picture? That's what happens when you focus on winning an argument but forget that God's model is for us to love one another: that's His big picture.

God's headline is that love should be the main focus. If your relationship is going to change then, selfishness needs to go. Loving your neighbour as yourself isn't just referring to the person who lives next door but also to the one who lives with you. Your spouse is your closest neighbour! Loving your spouse as yourself will mean a priority shift.

Verse 15 shows us the consequence, in the area of our communication, if we don't make that change. The words bite, devour and destroy are pretty strong, but we see many couples do just that.

Sarah and Andrew had a pattern of pulling each other down,

snapping at each other and taking bites out of each other's character. While taking every opportunity to say harsh words, they both complained that they didn't feel loved or respected. It was evident that it was love and respect they craved, but their communication style had set them on the road to a marriage in tatters. Their story didn't stop there because while God paints a vivid picture of what selfishness can do in relationships, He provides a way of turning things around and a pattern to live by.

> **Those who belong to Christ Jesus
> have crucified the flesh with its passions and desires.
> Since we live by the Spirit,
> let us keep in step with the Spirit.
> Galatians 5:24-25 NIV**

The body (the flesh) needs to be crucified but so do the passions and desires. Those passions (emotions) and desires (the will) are the parts that we need to tune out. We need to stop listening to our body and soul and start living by the Spirit.

For Andrew and Sarah, their tipping point was realising the damage that they were doing to one another and their relationship. Acknowledging the destruction also meant starting a journey of discovery. They both had to find out why they were trapped in a cycle of dysfunction. Andrew found this process easier than Sarah, his childhood had been far from pleasant, and he had witnessed his father behaving the same way to his mother as Andrew was acting in his relationship with Sarah. His childhood home had been filled with sarcasm, criticism and lack of respect. In the cold light of day he could acknowledge that this wasn't good for their relationship nor was it godly. He cringed as he remembered the obscene language he had first heard from the mouth of his father but which frequently peppered his own angry outbursts.

Sarah didn't have an obvious 'go to' when she examined her

patterns of behaviour. Her childhood home had been relatively peaceful, and disputes were handled in a civilised way. She didn't have a poor relationship with her siblings or a negative school experience, but she had had a previous boyfriend who had put her down and belittled her. When that relationship ended Sarah vowed that she would never let someone walk over her again. When Andrew and Sarah had their first fight, she felt as though she had been slapped verbally, she hadn't seen this side of Andrew before they got married. Determined to change things she decided to give as good as she got, and she did.

Both Andrew and Sarah realised that while there seemed to be good reasons for their behaviour, they need to take responsibility for their actions. As they both prayed and asked God to help them change, hope started to grow. They knew that they weren't on their own in the process but that God had given them the pattern and the power to change.

Over to You!

- *Do your words, actions and attitudes demonstrate that you love your spouse more than you love yourself?*
- *What patterns can you identify in your communication?*
  - *Where did they originate?*
  - *When did they originate?*
- *Take a few moments to bring those patterns to God and ask Him to exchange them for His pattern of communication.*

#marriagetip

When you find yourself in 'bite and devour' mode, then 'bite your tongue'. Ask for time out so you can think about why you are responding that way and ask God to show you what's going on emotionally that you feel the need to hurt your spouse with your words. Don't be afraid to ask for outside help, you might need a counsellor to help you walk through the healing of past wounds.

The Power to Change

So I say, walk by the Spirit,
and you will not gratify the desires of the flesh.
For the flesh desires what is contrary to the Spirit,
and the Spirit what is contrary to the flesh.
They are in conflict with each other,
so that you are not to do whatever you want.
But if you are led by the Spirit, you are not under the law.
Galatians 5:16-18 NIV

If you were to ask us what one thing has made the difference to the couples who we have helped over the years, it's this principle: learning to walk by the Spirit. It's not a one-time thing, it takes daily practice.

When God's Spirit works on your spirit, you start to gain victories over your selfishness. Instead of letting your mouth take the lead by saying the wrong thing, or your body take charge by doing the wrong thing, you allow God's spirit to guide you. It's clear that the spirit winning over the flesh is a battle, but the secret isn't in making it a law, the secret is in walking close to the Holy Spirit. Being willing to be led by Him in your actions, in your responses, and in your communication is key to gaining ground. Your words, attitudes and actions coming into subjection to the Holy Spirit will transform you.

This change doesn't come from your own effort. Like us, you've probably found it's not worked out too well when you're trying to do something in your own strength or by sheer willpower. You might understand what needs to change in your life but struggle not to fall back into old habits and patterns. When you walk by the Spirit, He moves on your spirit which touches the soul, which changes your actions rather than the body or the flesh having free reign.

When you journey through life with the help and guidance of the Holy Spirit, He will enable you in areas in which you felt incapable. In your communication, He is able to give you the empathy you lack or remove the fears you might have that cause you to react negatively. He gives you the words to build each other up instead of tearing each other down. He provides you with the ability to give the 'soft answer' which can calm an argument. In fact, all the things you need to develop your communication with each other come from being led by the Spirit. His Word makes it clear that you can be in control of your responses.

Andrew said that breaking the cycle of verbal abuse wasn't easy. He especially found it challenging if Sarah wanted to talk to him about something the moment he got home from work or when he was particularly stressed. What worked best was being given a heads up that they needed to talk so that he had time to get prepared mentally, emotionally and spiritually. Finances were always a significant area of contention for them, so they were both cautious about revisiting discussions about money. Andrew prayed and asked God to help him discuss their money problems with Sarah without it coming across as though he was blaming her. He realised that he had fallen into that trap in the past and discussions hadn't been a discussion but an opportunity to make accusations. He asked God to help him forgive Sarah for any financial decisions she had made in the past that he blamed her for.

When it came time to discuss the problems Andrew started at that point and apologised for the way that their discussions had gone in the past. He asked Sarah if she would forgive him, but he could tell by Sarah's face that this wasn't an easy thing for her to do. He realised that the conversation wouldn't go well until she had been able to process what he'd just said so he suggested she spent time with God too. He didn't get the reaction he had hoped for, Sarah left the room, and as she retreated to their bedroom, she slammed the door.

Sarah said it took about fifteen minutes for her temper to cool down. She felt insulted that Andrew had asked her to pray, she again felt like he was blaming her. Slowly she realised that he was really trying to do this differently, so she started to pray. God began to speak to her that she had been less than honest about what she spent and frequently hid purchases like the new shoes sitting at the back of the cupboard. He showed her that her sensitivity was because she felt guilty and her reactions weren't all Andrew's fault. In that bedroom Sarah forgave Andrew, but she was anxious about the conversation she knew they needed to have. As she opened her Bible, her eye fell on a highlighted section. 1 Peter 5:7 "Cast all your anxiety on him because he cares for you." She knew God was encouraging her, that He loved her and that He would help them as she brought her concerns to Him.

The conversation that followed was the most honest conversation they'd ever had about finances. They were both surprised at the relief they felt as both confessed some retaliation spending that had been going on. Instead of the usual reactions which sabotaged any ability to find a solution they were able to talk to each other about financial decision making and agreed that instead of hiding spending, or just informing each other about what they spent they'd make a budget and stick to it.

God gave them the power to change because they were willing to submit to Him.

Over to You!

- *Can you recognise times when you've been in conflict with one another because you're doing what you know God wouldn't want you to do?*
- *Are there any words you use, or names that you call your spouse which are not godly?*
- *Are there any subjects which you both find particularly difficult to talk about?*

- *Spend some time with God asking Him to show you what needs to change in your communication and allow Him to bring about the change you need.*

#marriagetip

As you try and implement change, you will probably find things don't always go well. Become aware of the 'triggers' that start your communication going downhill. Investigate why that trigger is there and ask for God's help to disarm it.

The Power of Communication

> "THE TONGUE HAS NO BONES BUT IS STRONG ENOUGH TO BREAK A HEART.
> SO BE CAREFUL WITH YOUR WORDS."
> UNKNOWN

How much thought do you put into choosing the words that you use with your spouse? The more comfortable you become in your relationship, the less guarded you tend to be. There can be many positives about letting down those guards, but it is essential that you learn to share your heart with the least amount of hurt, humiliation, or harm.

Our brains have an incredible ability to select from tens of thousands of words. By age four most of us know 5,000 words, by age eight that number has doubled, and most adults have a range of 20,000 - 35,000 words. That's a phenomenal amount of vocabulary we can use, and yet most of us speak without realising we have a choice of what to say.[7] The fact is that you do! You have a choice about what comes out of your mouth, but it means slowing down a little and employing your brain before you deploy your tongue. As someone who likes to deal with situations quickly, I've found that I've had to learn the hard way to stop, pray and consider what I'm going to say especially if I need to speak to Roy about an issue between us. In my zeal for sorting out a situation, I've often been rash and rushed in 'all guns blazing' only to find that I've caused wounds in the process. Do you have the same tendency?

> **There is one whose rash words are like sword thrusts,**
> **but the tongue of the wise brings healing.**
> **Proverbs 12:18 (ESV)**

Slowing down, asking God to help me see the situation from His perspective, asking Him to help me deal with my emotions and praying for wisdom regarding what to say, has always had a healthier outcome.

---

[7] https://www.economist.com/blogs/johnson/2013/05/vocabulary-size

Proverbs 12:18 contrasts two types of people, the rash and the wise. Saying something without careful consideration, of how those words might hurt, is not the wisest approach. I can attest to that. Maybe like me you can look back at arguments and wish you could 'un-say' some things. You too can identify that some of the things you've said to each other haven't been wise. You can't change the past but you can change how you communicate today. Maybe today can mark the beginning of detoxing your tongue?

When Your Tongue Needs Detoxing.

When you hear the word detox in the context of your tongue your mind might automatically jump to getting a 'swear box' and paying a fine. However, detoxing your tongue is not just about getting rid of curse words from your vocabulary, it's about overhauling your speech. This is necessary because there is a lot more power in words than you might think.

**Death and life are in the power of the tongue,
and those who love it will eat its fruits.
Proverbs 18:21 (ESV)**

Words aren't neutral or innocent, words are powerful. They can bring life, or they can be toxic, poisonous and bring death. Now, if the average person speaks 11 million words a year and most of the words that tumbled from their lips are negative or critical, you can imagine the impact that would have. This verse in Proverbs is a strong message from God to help us realise the importance of our words on those around us and on our own lives. It's clear that words can be used for good and can be used for harm. In fact, life and death are pretty heavy-duty words. If we realised that our words were that powerful would we be more careful with what we say? Our words not only affect other people but they also affect us, 'those who love it will eat its fruits.'

> "WORDS ARE SEEDS THAT DO MORE THAN BLOW AROUND.
> THEY LAND IN OUR HEARTS AND NOT THE GROUND.
> BE CAREFUL WHAT YOU PLANT AND CAREFUL WHAT YOU SAY.
> YOU MIGHT HAVE TO EAT WHAT YOU PLANTED ONE DAY."
> UNKNOWN

> **"I tell you that on the day of judgment people will have to account for every careless word they speak."**
> **Matthew 12:36 HCSB**

These are Jesus' words. It's not just talking about swear words, or every word that is used in anger, or gossip or nasty words but it says we will have to give an account for every 'careless' word. That means that we have to start taking what we say more seriously.

If you have ever been to a war museum, you might have seen a poster of a sinking ship with the words 'a few careless words may end in this' underneath it. The saying, 'Careless words sink ships' was used to try and remind people that their chatter might do some harm to others. Sometimes I think it would be worth having a poster of a couple sinking with the caption 'a few careless words may end in this'.

It's important that we think about what we are saying, the effect it has on other people and the effect it has on us. Perhaps you've been conscious about what you say to friends, or to your children but you haven't thought much about what you say to your spouse. Words carry so much power that the consequences for carelessness are pretty heavy. Imagine having to account for every careless word you use!

> Set a guard over my mouth, LORD;
> keep watch over the door of my lips.
> Psalm 141:3 NIV

This prayer was written by someone who knew his mouth could get him into a lot of trouble. In Psalm 39 David also uses the imagery of appointing a guard or watchmen to keep his tongue in check and expands his description to, 'I will guard my mouth with a muzzle'.

Have you ever walked past an aggressive dog? They can be pretty scary and intimidating! As horrible as they look muzzles have been designed to keep an animal from hurting others, the muzzle stops them from resorting to their usual mode of operation. Even if they snarl a bit, they can't do as much damage as they would want to. Often we don't even realise the damage our tongues can do. As children we used to sing 'sticks and stones will break our bones, but words will never harm us'. What a lie! Words can cause a lot of hurt. That's why David talks about holding back from saying what he really wants to say.

We probably are less guarded about the words we use when we are at home. The wrong thing can pour out of our mouths when we are with our spouse or our family. We might have had a rough day at work and when we come home our irritation that we held back all day spills out from unguarded lips. Wouldn't we be a lot more careful about what we say if there was someone on patrol listening to everything that came out of our mouths? We would think before we speak. Often we talk, and it doesn't even seem that we've engaged our brains. Our mouths are working all on their own! Unguarded, unchecked and unmuzzled.

Think about it for a moment, what do you think the Lord would stop you from saying? Can you imagine the difference this alone would make in your daily communication with your spouse?

Even when we are conscious of the power of our words, some words slip past the guard. We need to be proactive and learn how to gain better control of our tongues. While we can focus on the 'guards' we can put on our tongue, maybe like David, we can adopt another approach too. We need to think about the right things, if we do then what comes out of our mouths won't be as ugly or dangerous.

> **Let the words of my mouth and the meditation of my heart**
> **Be acceptable in Your sight,**
> **O Lord, my rock and my Redeemer.**
> **Psalm 19:14 ESV**

Over to You!

- *Is this an area you need to improve?*
- *What strategies have you used to guard your mouth?*
- *Are your words toxic (whether it's swearing or name-calling or being critical)?*
- *Do you need to detoxify your speech?*

#marriagetip

Start to pray Psalm 141:3 Set a guard over my mouth, LORD; keep watch over the door of my lips. As you memorise this scripture it will come back to you when you need that guard.

The Difference between Constructive and Destructive Communication

We probably all agree that communication falls mainly into two categories, constructive or destructive. You might argue that we have a third neutral category, but the Bible is more black and white than that and simply divides words in two. We're going to take a more in-depth look at what makes a marriage grow or what makes it shrivel up and die. Having heard the terms 'constructive' and 'destructive' misused many times by couples we have worked with, it might be time for a basic English lesson.

Constructive:

adjective
having or intended to have a useful or beneficial purpose.
"constructive advice"

synonyms: positive, useful, of use, helpful, encouraging
antonyms: destructive, negative

Destructive:

adjective
1. causing great and irreparable damage.
"the destructive power of weapons"

synonyms: devastating, ruinous, disastrous, catastrophic, calamitous, cataclysmic
antonyms: non-violent, creative

2. negative and unhelpful.
"destructive criticism"

synonyms: negative, hostile, antagonistic
antonyms: constructive

Unfortunately, when people think of the word constructive they often pair it with the word criticism. The term 'constructive criticism' is the one that generally is the most misused. Under that banner, many people feel justified in launching an all-out assault on their spouse; the result is the very opposite of constructive. Constructive criticism is supposed to be used to help to improve something, and it should aim to develop, advance or promote; so on the surface level it can seem reasonable. The reality is that in marriage, most people use the criticism tool without the 'constructive' attachment. Instead of building they damage, instead of constructing a healthy relationship they deconstruct it.

There is an old joke about marriage that goes like this: Men have often been puzzled by the change that occurs in their wives after marriage. They couldn't understand the transformation from love and adoration to criticism and dissatisfaction after the wedding day. A social scientist had an 'aha' moment when he attended a wedding and arrived at a logical reason for this metamorphosis. It all boiled down to a conditioning process as she walked down the aisle towards the altar. As she walked down the aisle on her father's arm, these three elements were reinforced: aisle, altar, hymn ... aisle, altar, hymn until she was fully conditioned to the thought 'I'll alter him'. Then looking up she sees the face of her groom and smiles as she thinks about how she will make that happen.

Unfortunately, many people enter marriage with the intention of improving the person that they have agreed to wed. I was one of them! One of the 'flaws' I thought Roy had was that he was introverted, something I felt that I could fix. I attempted this in lots of ways, we went out to social functions and to visit friends. I kept our schedule busy to give him the practice that I thought he lacked. He had no idea that this was my intention, but the busyness of our lives was taking its toll. He put his foot down and said we ought to stay home more. My manipulative ways kicked in, so I kept inviting people over instead, after all, he still needed the practice (or so I thought). As an out and out extrovert I had no idea what impact that had on Roy and how exhausted social interaction, in that capacity, made him feel. I gave up this false quest feeling like a failure and also disappointed that Roy wasn't willing to change.

It was a few years later that I eventually learned that being introverted didn't mean Roy was damaged or broken, he didn't need to be fixed or improved, he needed a wife who understood. I also grew to understand myself more. I discovered that the reason why I felt the need to re-educate Roy was because I felt lonely. Gary Chapman puts it like this, "People tend to criticise their spouse most loudly in the area where they themselves have the deepest emotional need." Instead of understanding and expressing my needs in a positive way I focused on Roy's 'flaws'. I attempted to give him a makeover and in the process conveyed the message that he wasn't good enough.

Constructive criticism is, for the most part, an oxymoron; it's difficult to build and tear down at the same time. In our case the years of undermining who Roy was as a person took their toll. I asked for forgiveness and Roy forgave me, but we needed to rebuild our relationship. It wasn't just Roy that I had torn down, our marriage had been impacted too, I was hurting myself.

A man who is kind benefits himself, but a cruel man hurts himself.
Proverbs 11:17 ESV

In case you walk away with the impression that you can never address the issues you have in your relationship, that's not the case. In this scenario, I had set out to fix what wasn't broken, but there were other areas in our relationship that needed to change. We'll talk about effective strategies for addressing issues later, but our point is that criticism should never be one of them.

Over to You!

- *Do you have a tendency to be critical of your spouse?*
- *What proportion/percentage of your thoughts concerning your spouse are negative?*
- *Do you recognise a desire to 'fix' your spouse?*
- *How do you receive criticism, do you feel it's constructive when it's directed at you?*

#marriagetip

Next time you are tempted to criticise your spouse pause and consider if there is something else going on. Is it possible you are lashing out at your spouse because of your own emotional need? If you have a need, expressing it in a healthy way is more likely to get you long lasting results than the short term change that criticism is likely to bring.

The Difference between Building Up and Tearing Down

Having dreams and vision beyond your wedding day is crucial. Most of us have already some aspirations in mind; they may include career, children and owning our own home. You may have a dream home in mind and are working towards the goal of purchasing it, but without a good marriage, that home becomes only a house. True construction means building; building a home for yourselves and building a healthy relationship. Constructing your real home should primarily focus on building your relationship. To do this effectively you need to follow Biblical principles.

> "Therefore encourage one another and build each other up, just as in fact you are doing."
> 1 Thessalonians 5:11 NIV

Interestingly the phrase 'build each other up' can also be translated as 'edify'. It comes from two Greek words: oikos which means 'a home' and dimeo which means 'to build'. It's important to realise that your home is less to do with a physical building and more to do with your relationships. Do you build up your spouse and your children or are you guilty of tearing them down?

Proverbs 14:1 contrasts two types of people, smart people and stupid ones.

> The wisest of women builds her house,
> but folly with her own hands tears it down.
> Proverbs 14:1 ESV

If we watched a couple physically building a home and then every time they had an argument they started tearing bricks out of the wall, we wouldn't consider them to be too smart. Unfortunately, negative communication does just this, it tears down what you have been trying hard to build.

Your home life might only be starting, you might be building from ground level if you have just got married and your relationship is in the early stages of growth. However, for those who have been married longer, it's just as important to put these principles into practice in your relationship. The word translated 'to build' is also relevant to restoration, rebuilding, repair and maintenance. That is good news for those who are struggling in their marriage and wondering how they are going to reverse their current situation and rebuild a broken relationship.

Where can you start? It is never too late to introduce encouragement into your marriage but if it hasn't been an established pattern you may find it difficult to know where to start.

> "Let no corrupting talk come out of your mouths,
> but only such as is good for building up, as fits the occasion,
> that it may give grace to those who hear."
> Ephesians 4:29 ESV

Encouragement is about supporting each other. If you go to watch sports, you usually go to cheer your team on rather than hurl abuse at them. To illustrate that what some of us think is encouraging is actually not, you only need to observe the behaviour of parents watching their children play a sport. We've heard parents name call, shout insults and shame their child in an effort to 'encourage' them to perform well. There is a huge difference between positive reinforcement and negative reinforcement. A parent, wanting to 'encourage' their child might say, 'I'll take you out after the game if you do well', alternatively they could say, 'You won't get to go out for a treat after the game if you do badly'. Both approaches are likely to motivate but the first is positive and the second is negative. The first is based on reward and the second is based on a threat, can you see the difference?

We see the same two tendencies in the couples we work with. For the most part (because the marriages we work with are often experiencing difficulty) we see negative reinforcement more often than positive reinforcement. Encouragement and threats don't walk hand in hand. Instead, cheer each other on in what you are doing, you are on the same side. A useful example of how we should support one another is to think of a candle in a candle holder. Without the candle holder, the candle can't stand and can't do its job effectively. Sometimes it's difficult to see your spouse's need for support, especially if they come across as strong and confident. Everyone needs to feel safe and secure in their relationship; that comes from being encouraged, supported, championed, and knowing that you have your spouse's backing in life.

Support is a human need; it isn't a weakness. If you've been guilty of tearing down rather than supporting, apologise for being negative. Repentance can be difficult especially if you feel justified in what you have said, but negativity sown in marriage is a destructive seed and will not yield a positive result.

If you don't think your spouse deserves encouragement be careful! Don't buy into the retaliation game. Too many people use the excuse "Why should I encourage them when they don't encourage me?". There is a spiritual law called sowing and reaping. Galatians 6:7 says "Do not be deceived, God is not mocked; for whatever a man sows this he will also reap". If you want to start receiving encouragement, then begin sowing it.

The first step might be as simple as learning to say thank you. Thank you may seem like an insignificant thing to say, but it means so much to the person who is hearing it. A sincere thank you given for mundane tasks, as well as for gifts, is an encouragement.

> "Anxiety in a man's heart weighs him down,
> but a good word makes him glad."
> Proverbs 12:25 ESV

Perhaps you don't have an issue encouraging your spouse, but you struggle to receive. If you have trouble accepting encouragement you need to realise that you are of value in God's eyes. Study these scriptures to see how He feels about you.

- You have value (Psalm 139:13-16).

- Christ loved you so much He died for you (Romans 5:8).

- You are God's own child (John 1:12).

- God has a plan and a purpose for your life (Ephesians 2:10).

OVER TO YOU!

Write down 5 things you appreciate about your spouse:

#marriagetip

If you are having difficulty doing this think about even the smallest of things. For example, you might appreciate being made a cup of coffee, the way they look, the help they are around the home. Once you start looking for the good in someone, the task becomes much easier. Often you can focus so hard on the negative that you forget about the positive attributes of your spouse.

The Difference between Salty and Sour Conversations

**Better is a dry morsel with quiet
than a house full of feasting with strife.
Proverbs 17:1 ESV**

Unhealthy communication in marriage makes you miserable. You may live in a beautiful home, have no financial worries, be surrounded by everything your heart desires, but without peace in the home, it is meaningless. We usually associate a 'dry morsel' with bread and water and being in jail, many couples joke about marriage being like a prison sentence. This verse tells us that actually being on bread and water would be far better than having to live in a home which is filled with conflict and friction. Poor communication affects the atmosphere around you turning even the most beautiful home into a frosty, heartless place.

**The beginning of strife is like letting out water,
so quit before the quarrel breaks out.
Proverbs 17:14 ESV**

This imagery is such a powerful description of what happens when an argument starts. Usually, people don't deal with only one thing, but they throw every hurt, disappointment and accusation at each other. Often they open up the history book of past offences and throw that too. If you've ever seen footage of a dam breaking and the water spewing out of every crack, it's a good reminder of the potentially destructive force of quarrelling. If you've not been communicating well, it's very possible that you've already stored up a dam full of offence. Understanding the potential for that dam bursting and washing away everything you've been trying to build is the first step in dealing with it. It's a little bit like completing a structural survey and looking for weaknesses in the dam wall. The next step is understanding what is likely to come out when you start communicating. Will it be sweet or sour?

> **But now you must put them all away:**
> **anger, wrath, malice, slander, and obscene talk from your mouth.**
> **Colossians 3:8 ESV**

Lainey:
I recently had to go to the doctor because I was having issues with my digestion. I couldn't stomach what I had been eating, and there were lots of consequences in my day to day life. The doctor told me that it was going to be necessary to do a complete cleanse and eliminate any foods which were irritating me. That wasn't something I wanted to hear because I didn't want to have to restrict my diet. I knew though that if I didn't change there would be negative consequences to my long-term health. We're asking something similar of you today. Colossians calls us all to action and tells us that we must get rid of the destructive things that come out of our mouths. What does that mean for you?

Colossians puts getting rid of anger and wrath (rage) right at the top of the list. Detoxing your heart of those emotions gets rid of the catalyst for malice, slander and obscene talk. If you don't deal with the soulish side, then you'll emotionally vomit over the people around you, and your feelings will pour out in the wrong way. The secret isn't just having good self-control it's asking the Holy Spirit to help you go against your natural tendencies in situations and to get God's heart for one another.

> HOLDING A GRUDGE DOESN'T MAKE YOU STRONG; IT MAKES YOU BITTER.
> FORGIVING DOESN'T MAKE YOU WEAK; IT SETS YOU FREE.
> DAVE WILLIS: 7 LAWS OF LOVE

There are significant benefits to getting your communication right. The advantage of learning to control what comes out of your mouth is having a life you love and good days ahead. Those are pretty nice rewards!

Right in the middle of Galatians 5 there is a long list of behaviours which are present when someone isn't walking by the Spirit. We can have a tendency to hone in on what we might consider the 'big issues' to be while skipping over those we think are 'insignificant'. It's especially tempting to ignore some of the actions or reactions that we are guilty of, specifically those in the area of communication. For that reason, we're going to focus in on the parts that are most relevant to destructive communication. The opening declaration of verse nineteen highlights that it should be obvious to us that these issues are from the flesh.

The acts of the flesh are obvious ...hatred, discord, jealousy, fits of rage, selfish ambition, dissensions, factions and envy;... I warn you, as I did before, that those who live like this will not inherit the kingdom of God.
Galatians 5:19-21 NIV

Is there evidence of 'the flesh' in your communication? Let's move through these, one by one. Hate is strong emotional language, especially when you compare it to the love that brought you together. Hate is usually the result of hurt, it's an expression of anger which has taken up residence in the heart. The swing in emotions for most couples isn't swift, it's most often a journey which takes time to accomplish. We've heard many couples argue and yell 'I hate you!', but usually they mean 'You hurt me to such a degree that I can't cope with being around you in case you hurt me again.' Deeper hate develops when arguments are unresolved, a cycle of hurt is established, and self-protection seems to be the only way forward. Hate is an inevitable result of destructive communication, it usually manifests in 'fits of rage'.

> **A hot-tempered person stirs up conflict,**
> **but the one who is patient calms a quarrel.**
> **Proverbs 15:18 NIV**

When you lose your temper, you've probably realised that it causes a reaction and that reaction isn't positive, it 'stirs up conflict'. Without realising the damage you're causing words spew out of your mouth, and those words go deep. Remember, words are not neutral, they have the power to hurt or the power to heal. Words used in anger or even in thoughtlessness can destroy people's identity. Learning how to communicate doesn't mean you suddenly magically agree on everything, but it does mean that you can diffuse rather than feed arguments.

When you shout, it sometimes sounds like you are talking to someone in the next city never mind the same room. It's almost like there is a massive distance between you, even if you are standing in close proximity to each other. In a sense, there is a distance, and that's because the distance is between your hearts.

Galatians 5 also lists the word discord in its list of destructive behaviours. Discord isn't a word that's used much today. It's a lack of harmony between two notes in music. When we hear someone singing off-key, or we hear music that doesn't sound as though it's in harmony, we are very quick to turn it off. Everything about discord grates on the nerves and makes the listener uncomfortable. Yet many homes open their doors and invite discord to stay. Strife, conflict, friction and hostility are invited to sit at the dining room table at meal times. Disunity and division send the couple in opposite directions, and ill-feeling encourages them to cling to their own side of the bed when they retire in the evening. When a couple operates with one-accord, there is no room for discord in their home.

> Complete my joy by being of the same mind, having the same love, being in full accord and of one mind.
> Philippians 2:2 ESV

Jealousy is another factor which contributes to destructive communication and turns a conversation sour. It can be grouped together with 'selfish ambition, dissensions, factions and envy' also mentioned in Galatians 5:19-21. Jealousy is often rooted in a feeling that something isn't fair. If you find yourself comparing workloads, contrasting abilities, and pointing out your spouse's weaknesses, it's possible that you feel a deep sense of injustice. When that need for justice or fairness isn't met, then it often manifests in a negative way through sour words and a sour attitude.

There is a vast contrast between the behaviours listed as 'fleshly' and what we see in a Spirit-led life.

> **But the fruit produced by the Holy Spirit within you is divine love in all its varied expressions: joy that overflows, peace that subdues, patience that endures, kindness in action, a life full of virtue, faith that prevails, gentleness of heart, and strength of spirit. Never set the law above these qualities, for they are meant to be limitless.**
> Galatians 5:22-23 TPT

In a Spirit-led life: hate is replaced by love, when discord leaves peace can take its place and fits of rage are no longer present, but self-control has been established. In contrast to living in a 'fleshly' way jealousy and selfish ambition are redundant as selflessness, kindness and goodness are put to work. Faithfulness and unity are present when dissensions and disunity are removed from the heart. When your heart towards God and towards each other is healed, then you can have grace towards one another. Your speech will also be transformed in the process.

> **Let your conversation be always full of grace, seasoned with salt, so that you may know how to answer everyone.**
> **Colossians 4:6 NIV**

Salt is a preservative, it stops things going off. In other words, it prevents things from going sour. Salt might not seem like much today since our homes are kitted out with refrigerators but in the past salt was something that was valued. Some time ago we had the fantastic opportunity to visit some salt mines in Poland. Before that experience, we had little idea just how important salt was. In the past salt wasn't readily available and took work to mine, so it was an expensive commodity. Owning a large, man-sized block of salt was the equivalent of being rich enough to own a village. We might not think much of it if we spill some salt, but back then it would have been considered a waste to use it unwisely.

I wonder what would happen if we started to value our words? Our words can be used to bless, to bring value to the people around us. If our words are seasoned with salt, they aren't going to be difficult for people to swallow. We can ask God for His help to 'purify' what comes out of our mouths so that it isn't something detrimental to our relationships. That means asking God to purify us from within, purifying our hearts as well as our words. It means making a transition from having 'tasteless' or sour conversations to having 'salty' conversations.

Salt also prevents the growth of microbes which can spoil food. In a sense salt changes the environment so that microbes, which cause diseases, simply can't flourish. It enhances the texture, flavour and colour of food, but what does all this mean for how you talk to one another? Remember we are body soul and spirit, so sometimes intellectualism, choices and emotions can derail a healthy conversation and spoil it. Having conversations which are lead by God's Spirit keeps them on track. He prevents microbes of offence, anger and hurt from flourishing. Not only that but God changes the way we talk, and what we talk about, He changes the texture, flavour and colour of our conversations.

In this verse Paul encourages us to fill our conversations with grace, that is the 'salt' that brings a different flavour to our homes. What does that mean in practical terms? Grace isn't something that we have a natural capability or capacity for. Grace flows from 'the divine influence upon the heart', as Strong's concordance puts it. When God influences us it pours out into our lives, we are able to live life with joy, liberty and gratitude. Instead of criticism 'seasoning' our words and souring our conversation grace is present instead.

Over to You!

- *Can you identify areas in your communication where you are letting the body or your soul lead?*

- *What would your communication look like if you always walked in the Spirit?*
    - *How would it change?*
    - *What one thing are you going to change to stop your emotions and selfishness from ruling your communication with each other?*

- *If you can see that the quality of your conversations could be improved are you willing to add a little salt?*

- *What could you talk about that would improve the flavour of your marriage?*

#marriagetip

When you start identifying areas in your communication which need to change it can seem a little overwhelming. Remember that the main thing you need to do is to walk by the Holy Spirit. When you do that He will lead and guide you to say and do the right thing.

The Need to Learn Your Spouse's Language

So far we've examined the reasons why getting communication right is essential. We've also taken a look at some of the challenges husbands and wives have in their conversation, simply because men and women are not wired the same way. Those differences are evident in most marriages where communication has been a struggle. It's wonderful that God wants to restore our ability to understand each other at a deeper level and that He has given us the tools to do that. He makes it clear that there is power in communication, and that power was designed for our good if we learn how to use language the way it was intended.

In marriage, you will always be 'the non-native speaker' simply because you don't speak the same 'language' as your spouse. It isn't solely because of gender differences but also because of your unique cultural approaches to life. Your love for your spouse should compel you to learn their way of communicating. The thing is though that we do need to learn. You can discover a lot about how to talk with your spouse if you approach it in the same way as you would approach learning a foreign language.

Rosetta Stone is one of the most well-known language learning tools in the world. It has an excellent reputation and has helped many people learn new languages, but there are things that Rosetta Stone simply can't teach you. So we are going to take some principles of language learning and push them a little further so that you are better equipped to understand your spouse.

What Rosetta Stone Can't Teach You

Language learning. What is your reaction to that phrase? For both of us, it's a term which can bring up all sorts of emotions including fear and a sense of inadequacy. Unless you are one of those supremely gifted in the art of language learning, you may have a similar reaction. The fact is that some people find language learning relatively easy and others find it supremely challenging. Which one are you?

Likewise, for any couple endeavouring to understand each other more fully, some will find it easier than others. When you attempt to learn your spouse's language, there are a few pitfalls you should try to avoid. You might have decided what you want to accomplish in communication, but it is vital that you communicate what you are trying to do and that your spouse is on board with the process. It's possible your spouse might feel like you're suddenly being pushy if you start organising times to chat or start to ask them questions you never have in the past. It may feel as though this is laborious and cumbersome but just like learning any language a lot of effort is needed if you are truly going to understand each other.

A linguist named Mark Manson explained how he searched and searched for language hacks. He wanted to find the shortcuts to easy communication and ease of language learning. This is what he concluded, "If there's a "secret" or "hack" to learning a new language, it's this: hours and hours of awkward and strenuous conversation with people better than you in that language."

We wish we could suggest a marriage hack to help you learn how to understand each other, but our conclusions are similar to Mark's.

You can't shortcut communication in a relationship. If you are really going to learn how to communicate effectively you will need to push through those awkward moments of misunderstanding, you will need to embrace the difficult conversations. Doing this will be easier for some personality types than for others, so be sensitive to your spouse.

Over to You!

It's also useful to understand your own approach to language learning. If you've already tried to learn another language then perhaps you can relate to some of the styles below. Which type of 'language learner' are you when it comes to speaking your spouse's language?

- *Do you give up before you start? When you hear that foreign tongue, it just flows over your head like gobbledygook, and you immediately decide that there is no point in trying. You can't even separate out the words, never mind connecting them into a meaningful sentence. You may acquire a few words which help you navigate. You know the easier words like yes, no or food. Obviously, if this is your default setting you're going to have to fight against your natural tendency and push through with learning how to communicate with your spouse. Do you keep speaking your own language ... just a little bit LOUDER? When you speak, you continue to use your language sometimes slowing it down to such a degree that your spouse thinks you're both in a foreign language sitcom. You may even try raising your voice in the hope that the volume will somehow flick a switch of understanding in your spouse's head. It usually flicks a switch alright, but it isn't one of understanding!*

- *Do you nod your head and pretend to understand more than you do? When you listen, you can identify a number of keywords in the sentence, so you get the gist of what the other person is talking about, but it doesn't always work. Sometimes you badly misunderstand and totally get the wrong point of the communication. Your spouse is even more frustrated because you nodded your head indicating that you understood. The result is that they think you purposefully do the opposite of what they asked you to do.*

- *Do you use the halfway there approach? When you speak, you use a mix between your own and your spouse's language. Sometimes they can guess the point of your communication especially if you wave your hands around while explaining. At other times they look at you as though you have lost it.*

- *Are you already fluent? When you listen you understand everything that is said and get it in the correct context. Warning! Even 'the fluent' can make mistakes. You can still misunderstand, use the wrong word or just not make sense of something, but life is much more manageable when it makes more sense. When you speak, your spouse understands what you are saying because you can articulate your feelings. Not just what they are but why you feel that way. Even better, they give you feedback so you get to understand them more!*

#marriagetip

Regardless of your past approach determine today to take some 'language lessons' and learn how to communicate well with your spouse! Do you need to change your approach to learning your spouse's language? If so, what obstacles do you need to overcome?

The Language of the Heart

Language programmes tend to concentrate on giving you new vocabulary, helping you construct sentences and teaching you grammar. They can help you acquire language, but they can't help you learn to understand the language of the heart. Heart language can only be learned through time, effort and the willingness to communicate at the deepest level. If you stop short, by only learning the superficial language of your spouse, you will fail to reach the deepest level of relationship, one that is achieved by communicating heart to heart. Whether you and your spouse share a native tongue is not the issue, it's whether or not you are able to communicate heart to heart.

A friend recently described to us the difficulties she has encountered when communicating across languages. She is fluent in English and is an excellent communicator, but she explained that the main problem she had was that English wasn't her heart language. That phrase stuck with me. She could express many things in English, but when it came to matters of the heart, it became more challenging to communicate effectively. Many couples experience the same difficulty. Men and women express their hearts in different ways. These differentiations are not just an issue for those with extreme cross-cultural backgrounds; gender differences create their own cross-cultural tensions.

A heart language, by definition, is one in which the person feels most comfortable, most fluent, most able to express what is going on emotionally. When communicating in marriage, it is vital that you are able to convey what is in your heart. Although language can prove to be a barrier that is difficult to climb over, you can help each other overcome any obstacles by getting better at translation.

Some people struggle to share their heart because they were not given the freedom to express their emotions when they were being raised. The underlying message they received was that it was wrong to have certain feelings. Anger, sorrow, frustration and even joy were things to be repressed not expressed.

Our mother tongue or heart language is also the one which provides a feeling of safety. We can trust our own language because we know exactly what that means, there is no ambiguity, no fear of poor translation. One of the things we have discovered in the process of learning Hungarian is that we don't feel safe. We know that we will very possibly miscommunicate, at 'worst' we could cause offence; at 'best' we could become the source of local entertainment. Since neither Roy nor I like to be the butt of jokes, even the 'best' option is unattractive. Simply put, communication requires risk and stepping out of the comfort zone.

Over to You!

- What was the cultural environment in your childhood home?
- Were there any emotions that you felt were wrong to express?
- When you're sharing with your spouse are there any specific feelings you find difficult to talk about?
- Do you feel understood by your spouse at heart level?
- Do you feel that you understand your spouse at heart level?

#marriagetip
Earlier in the book we talked about the desire to belong, the desire for friendship, intimacy and unity. Being able to relate to each other 'heart to heart' is the way in which you will have that need met and be able to meet that need for your spouse. If sharing your heart doesn't come naturally for you or your spouse remember the journey is filled with tiny steps, not just one great leap.

Topical and Relational Communication

Roy and I used to get frustrated when our communication would end up in miscommunication. We often were bewildered when we would try and work out what had gone wrong. We frequently got our wires crossed and got 'static' on the line. Roy felt I was misquoting him while I would remain convinced of what I believed he had said. Old wounds would also feed into the miscommunication creating more misunderstanding. It's possible that you too may be frustrated because your discussions end up in arguments and you don't have a clue why they always reach that point. Did you know that it is possible that you are not really talking about the topic you think you are talking about?

The following revelation helped us untangle the mess we made of our communication and start understanding each other correctly. A 'topical' or 'head' statement filtered through 'relational' or 'heart' glasses can be interpreted as something entirely different. You may think you are talking about the house, the car, an item of clothing or a meal and your spouse may believe you are talking about his or her value, worth or lack of ability.

Let's start by defining what topical and relational communication are. Many years ago, Roy and I attended a seminar by Craig Hill. He shared the concept of topical and relational communication and, in the process, unlocked a mystery which had been plaguing us. In the past, I often felt that Roy really wasn't listening to me or understanding what I was trying to tell him. From Roy's perspective, he could never understand why I would react emotionally when we were talking about facts. What neither of us realised was that there were two different types of communication which were inhibiting our ability to understand each other.

Topical communication focuses on the facts. A fact may be that you don't have enough money in the bank or that you are tired. The topical communicator may be astounded to discover that their spouse isn't receiving those facts well; in fact, they are upset and angry. Logically the topical communicator reinforces why there is not enough money in the bank, or they might explain what has made them feel tired. When their spouse gets even more irate, the topical communicator is at a complete loss as to why their spouse is unable to understand their point of view. Voices often rise to emphasise the point (Roy's speciality), and the argument escalates.

What went wrong? The topical communicator didn't realise that while they only intended to send a factual message, a relational message was delivered as well. "We don't have enough money" could be interpreted relationally as: "You spend too much", "You're not worth it", "You don't work hard enough". "I'm tired" may be translated as: "I don't want to spend time with you", "You are a low priority" or "I work harder than you".

Topical communication is talking about particular themes; this includes not only neutral objects but can include talking about the kids or where to go on holiday. You may think you are solely relating on a 'topical' level, but you can be sure that other depths of communication are being touched on. Arguments rarely are the result of the topic – they are usually the result of a relational message that has been received.

It can take a little time and effort to overcome misunderstandings that arise from the topical and relational communication styles, but it is well worth the effort. Now, if I have any concerns about what Roy is trying to communicate I take time to 'translate' for him the relational message that I received. Roy is often bewildered by how what he innocently said could possibly be interpreted in such a negative way. I have learned to trust that when he says, 'That's not what I meant.' that statement is absolutely true.

Over to You!

- *If you start arguing, stop and ask your spouse what they heard (N.B. not what you said but what they understood).*

- *If you have hurt them, don't justify yourself, apologise.*

- *Explain that you were relating on the topical level and that they are very much valued.*

- *Give each other permission to ask for clarification. (When you said "this" I understood "that" is that what you intended to communicate?).*

- *Trust your spouse when they explain their heart.*

- *Give up any resentment you may be holding on to.*

#marriagetip

When you are responding to your spouse make sure that you are gentle rather than harsh.

**A gentle tongue is a tree of life,
but perverseness in it breaks the spirit.
Proverbs 15:4 ESV**

The Comfort of the Mother Tongue

I have discovered that one of the things I enjoy most about returning either to Northern Ireland or England is that I can fully relax. I feel equally at home in both places. It is almost like settling into a comfortable old armchair, I know all the shapes and contours, I have a place moulded for me which fits perfectly, there is no discomfort or awkward readjustments. When I speak my 'native' language, it's just like that. I know all the idiosyncrasies and nuances of those dialects. I can joke without fearing that the joke will be misunderstood because I understand the sense of humour. I can follow conversations without effort because I also appreciate the culture and therefore get the context of the subject. My heart feels like it has returned home and I feel at peace.

Ironically language can either be an aid or an obstacle to communication. We've already talked about some of the differences in how communication typically happens for men and women. In normal language learning circumstances, we use the term 'mother tongue'. Your mother tongue is your default language; it's the language you return to when you can't find adequate words. When you are expressing yourself in your mother tongue, you'll use phrases which are natural to you. Expressions that perfectly convey what you mean and are understood by those who have the same mother tongue.

Over the years we have worked with many marriages. Often someone will try and express something important to them. Since we work with many cross-cultural couples, we've frequently experienced someone burst out in their native tongue what they really want to say. They then try and double back and 'translate' their words. They struggle with what they view as an inadequate translation for what was really on their heart. There simply isn't an alternative word or phrase which explains their thoughts as well as a particular word or phrase in their mother tongue. Men and women alike can feel frustrated when their spouse doesn't understand what they felt they communicated really clearly. It's likely that they did communicate clearly but in their 'mother-tongue'.

As a foreigner living on Hungarian soil, I am often asked what my mother tongue is. I, of course, could reply that it is English, but I know that doesn't quite explain it. That explanation stops short of giving an accurate representation of my language and my funny accent. English is the primary language of many nations, but in each place, it develops and is used differently, often to the point that it causes as much confusion as a foreign language.

I am aware that my speech has changed over the years. I was born in Northern Ireland and had a strong mid-Ulster accent well into my early twenties. Marrying an Englishman left an impression on my speech which still results in the light-hearted sneers of my fellow countrymen when they call me "the Englishwoman". My husband and I moved from Northern Ireland to the North West of England where I took on board some wonderful 'northernisms'. I progressed from 'wetting the tea' to 'brewing' it and from making a sandwich to making a 'butty'. When we moved to the U.S.A. my speech adapted further and a few 'Americanisms' were thrown into the melting pot. My mother tongue, therefore, isn't pure but neither is Roy's. His language base comes from the Midlands, Australia, Wales, Northern Ireland and America. Nevertheless, the hotchpotch of backgrounds has made it a little more complex to discern the meaning behind the words; our speech is interwoven not only with a number of dialects but with a myriad of cultures. Our language is only the same at surface level.

You can easily see the possible miscommunication problems that can arise whether from the differences in heart language, topical and relational communication or family culture. If you find yourself frequently disagreeing but not understanding why, then it's worth investigating if you have really understood what they are saying. You can use this process to help unpick why you may have misunderstood your spouse.

Over to you!

- Did you understand their heart?
- What was the topical message?
- What did you understand the relational message to be?
- What relational message did they intend to send? (Don't guess, ask them).
- Are there any words or phrases that trigger arguments?
- Do you have the same definition of those words?
- Are there any negative associations with those words?

#marriagetip

If you find that there is confusion over a word or phrase then it's worth asking, 'What does that phrase mean to you'? You can eliminate a lot of confusion by being willing to see that what you think you understand might have another interpretation. You have a wonderful opportunity to get to know each other at a whole new level. When you begin to understand your spouse's mother tongue you are a language master.

The Funny Side of Life

Rosetta Stone can't teach you how to 'get' a joke. Understanding all the words in a sentence does not mean you will understand a culture's humour. Humour is a key component of any healthy relationship. Being able to laugh and have fun together alleviates the tensions of the day and brings you closer. The problem with humour is that it isn't something that easily crosses borders. What one country will find hilarious, another country finds offensive. The same can be said for closer cultural borders such as the differences between how you were raised. Humour can be a minefield in any marriage with the dangers being hidden until you step on the explosive. Both spouses can become shell-shocked, one because they can't believe their spouse would find something like that funny, and the other because their spouse can't understand their sense of humour.

In my home culture, our sense of humour drips with sarcasm. The Northern Irish are known for their quick wit but their sense of humour, while mostly self-deprecating can also be very sarcastic. For those from a country which celebrates its sarcastic sense of humour, there is little sympathy for those who don't get the joke. For those from a non-sarcastic culture, sarcasm is deemed the lowest form of humour, and there is very little respect for those who indulge in it. We hadn't been married for too long before my sarcasm started having an adverse effect on our relationship. I always had a quick comeback for Roy when he said something, and I found it very amusing, (intended emphasis on the word I!) What I considered to be witty comments, Roy deemed to be hurtful. Roy could not see the funny side. After defending my sense of humour and telling him that he didn't have a funny bone in his body, I started to think about what I was doing. It wasn't a 'who is right?' and 'who is wrong?' type of situation, I had to look at it from the perspective of what was right for our marriage.

> "The wise woman builds her house,
> but with her own hands the foolish one tears hers down."
> Proverbs 14:1 NIV

We referred to this scripture when we talked about the need to build up rather than tear down and it's worth using it again here. In defending my sense of humour and my culture I was actually tearing down something that I held dear, my husband and my home. That was a difficult pill to swallow! I had to make a choice and that day I chose to build my home rather than to tear it down. I asked God to put a guard on my mouth so that I wouldn't automatically say the words that came so quickly to my brain. Over a period of time, I found that I could express my sense of humour in other ways which didn't involve tearing my husband to shreds.

Richard and Maria Kane (founders of Marriage Week International) often teach that humour is the 6th language of love. There is a lot of truth in that statement. Having a good sense of humour is a blessing when you are learning to communicate. We've often found that a conversation that could have ended in disaster turns a corner when we choose to see the funny side of our mistakes. I appreciate Roy's sense of humour, his dry comments, his 'Dad' jokes (which he enjoys more than anyone else in the family) and his lighthearted rhetoric on life. Life is much fuller when it's fun!

Over to You!

- *Do you share your spouse's sense of humour?*
- *Is there anything about your sense of humour that hurts or wounds your spouse?*
- *Is there anything your spouse finds funny that wounds you?*
- *Do you laugh together (rather than at one another)?*

- *When was the last time you took time out to have fun together?*

#marriagetip

While many changes have been unconscious and natural, there have been a number of changes which have been consciously made. If I have identified a habit or a mannerism that has irritated my husband I have endeavoured to change. Those changes have not always been easy, and I have found myself on my knees asking God for help. If you are struggling to break a deeply ingrained habit, don't be discouraged. It's a matter of prayer and daily choices.

The Enigma Machine

You may recognise the name 'The Enigma Machine' either from your history lessons or by movies of that name. The Enigma Machine was an invention by the German engineer Arthur Scherbius who came up with the concept at the end of World War I. It was a machine that was used to encrypt and decrypt messages. As long as the allies went without the knowledge needed to break the codes, the garbled messages that the machine produced left them scratching their heads.

In marriage, you can feel very much the same way about what your spouse communicates. A message is sent but to the opposite sex, receiving that message, it seems as though it is encrypted. Confusion and frustration result and you are left wondering how you can break the code and understand each other.

> "The single biggest problem in communication
> is the illusion that it has taken place".
> George Bernard Shaw

Many messages which passed back and forth, in a time of war, made sense on one level but had a whole other level of meaning that was hidden. These messages could only be deciphered by someone who firstly knew there was a hidden message and secondly had the means and ability to extract it. Perhaps you have felt that you have been communicating clearly and are struggling to understand why your spouse looks at you with a blank expression. Have you considered that you have your own, personal, specific code that you insert into the words and phrases you use? To your ears, your conversation is loaded with meaning, but if your spouse doesn't understand what you are telling them, then communication has not taken place.

Something as innocent as planning a date can demonstrate the form that these messages sometimes appear in. We're going to ask you to imagine the following scene but to place yourself in a husband's shoes. (easy if you're the husband reading this but more challenging if you are a wife - it's all about empathy!) Let's say you're choosing a movie to watch. Your 'wife' suggests a mushy romantic film that you aren't too keen on. In turn, you suggest an action-packed movie which has caught your eye. Your spouse goes along with your suggestion but as the evening continues you start to realise that all is not well on the home front. You ask why your spouse is upset and you are bewildered when she says that you never take her into consideration in your decisions about movies. All this time you're thinking 'Of course I do!' so you explain that you asked her what she wanted to watch and you both came to the decision to watch the action movie. As your spouse vigorously shakes her head you wonder what on earth has gone wrong, you heard her agree to your suggestion. Your spouse then tells you that she told you what she wanted to watch, but you refused. Now you feel indignant! Your wife did not say she wanted to watch that movie, she suggested a few but didn't ever say, 'I really want to watch that one'.

What went wrong? There were probably a lot of clues along the way that were conveying a hidden message. A message which she felt she was conveying just as strongly as if she came right out and said it. Clues in her tone, her body language and not just in what she said. Most husbands don't deliberately ignore what their partner is communicating; rather they just don't catch that there is another less obvious level of meaning.

It's time to take the enigma out of marriage and understand how to break those codes.

How to Code Break

"COMMUNICATION IS WHAT IS HEARD, NOT ONLY WHAT IS SAID OR WRITTEN. CULTURAL PATTERNS OF A SOCIETY FUNDAMENTALLY INFLUENCE THE FORM OF COMMUNICATION. EXISTING BELIEFS AND VALUE SYSTEMS ARE A MAJOR FACTOR IN BUILDING COMMUNICATION. PERSONALITY AND EXPERIENCE MODIFY THE FORM OF THE MESSAGE".
REV. DR ARNE H. FJELDSTAD 'THE CONCEPT OF HEART LANGUAGE'

When Roy and I teach couples about communication, we teach about the filters each of us have which distort the words we receive. Those filters may be cultural, but they may also be because of hurts or experiences of the past. They can garble communication so severely that it would need a code breaker to sort out the confusion.

Imagine you are standing opposite one another and your spouse speaks to you. What they are communicating doesn't go straight from their head to your head, nor does it go straight from their heart to your heart. Instead, the message goes via a filter. If you can, visualise the filter as a large glass barrier between the two of you which diffracts or skews the message. For anyone who did light experiments at school, you probably have a very clear image now of the distortion this can bring. Now imagine that as your words pass through this barrier the meaning of some of those words change and distort.

The key to breaking the code is to listen carefully to the message that was received rather than concentrating on the message you thought you sent. If you can identify the words that have a distorted meaning when your spouse hears them, then you can begin to break the code. It's not as difficult as it might sound to do this. Some words will act like triggers which upset your spouse. Your spouse might suddenly become quiet or sullen, or they might become angry and upset. You can ask them 'What did I say that upset you?' You might be shocked when you hear words that you did not utter coming back to you. This is not the time to call them a liar! This is the time to realise you've just recognised a filter and now that it has been exposed you can act to deconstruct it. That means that you need to become skilled at identifying any significant reactions and asking questions to check your understanding.

You might be asking yourself where the ultimate responsibility lies for deconstructing filters. Does it belong to you or to your spouse? Filters are unlikely to be shared. Imagine a couple standing face to face, in between them are walls of filters. The wife will have her filters, and the husband will have his. The walls may differ in nature, but they both alter what the other one hears. If you agree to work together to improve your communication, then you can agree on two things. Firstly, that you are willing to have the truth of your filters challenged. If something that you have believed is not true of your spouse, then be prepared to drop that judgement. Secondly, you can help each other to recognise when the message you intended has become distorted. You can discuss what put that filter in place and respond with empathy rather than defensiveness. That barrier might have been there since childhood, or it might be something you have contributed to. If you have had a part in building it remember to apologise sincerely. Pray with your spouse as both of you work on removing your filters, ask God for His help to see the truth and to learn to trust one another.

Over to You!

- *Can you recognise any trigger words (tones or actions) in your communication with your spouse?*
- *What is the filter that those words pass through? Here are a few we've seen in relationships:*
    - *Negative - only translating your spouse's statements in a negative light.*

- *Black and white thinking - Seeing things in terms of extremes rather than in grey. Your spouse either loves you or hates you, thinks you are fantastic or horrible. Always and never statements are generally present when black and white thinking is in place.*

- *Overgeneralization - When you take a small problem that your spouse has mentioned and believe that your relationship is now at an end.*

- *Why is that filter in place? Culture, family habits, childhood hurts etc.*

- *Do you want that filter to remain?*

#marriagetip

The last question in the "Over to You!" section is the most significant. Identifying your filters but allowing them to remain unchallenged will continue to allow the messages you hear to be distorted. This, in turn, has an impact on your reactions. Having code-breaking skills is good, getting rid of the Enigma Machine is even better. You can choose to break down the filters of confusion.

Telepathic Delusions

One of the greatest myths about communication, which the media has been happy to reinforce, is the telepathic myth. Modern propaganda will tell you that your spouse should be so in tune with you that they will know what you need instinctively. They have somehow a connection with your mind which means that little communication is necessary and that you can live in harmony because you are 'soul mates'. Finding each other was like finding the other part of you and since you were 'meant to be' there should be no need for cumbersome communication. Such romantic drivel has been the death knell to many relationships. Don't fall for that lie!

The reality is that communication takes work and it takes work from both of you. Ladies, I think it is only right that I address some issues from one woman to another. We have often fallen into the trap of believing that our husbands should be able to read our minds. Have you ever subjected your husband to a game of charades when you have been upset with him?

Charades is a guessing game which, in a marriage, goes a little like this. Your husband comes home to be greeted by silence and a tense atmosphere, which is his signal that the game has begun.

There are three main husband types:

1. The skilled charades player. He asks the compulsory first question, "Are you okay dear?" to which you give the standard response, "I'm fine". At this point, he will realise that further questions are necessary because he will have correctly interpreted "I'm fine" as meaning "I am really mad with you".

2. The unskilled charades player. If your unsuspecting husband is not

a skilled charades player and he missed the first clue that the game had started. He may require the banging of cupboard doors or pots and pans to recognise that the game has begun. He blunders his way through and gets every clue wrong causing you more frustration.

3. The 'I won't play this game' player. He knows the game has begun the moment he walked in the door. Having played the game before and knowing that he had no hope of winning he simply chooses not to play. He exits the room, switches on the T.V. and puts his feet up. The wife attributes their marital problems to his poor communication skills.

Wives let's stop playing charades. Let's recognise the "I'm fine" routine for what it really is! When we say "I'm fine" but inside we are hurting, we are lying. How can we possibly expect our husbands to understand what is going on in our hearts if we refuse to communicate correctly? Blaming your spouse for poor communication is foolish when we refuse to explain the situation well. Simply put: if we choose to indulge in the charades game we will both come out losers.

Let's get rid of the idea that our husbands should instinctively know what we are thinking, what we are feeling or what we need. True communication starts with honesty, not with a guessing game. Say what you mean and mean what you say.

Although this section has been addressed to wives, we both recognise that it's not always the case that it's the wife who leaves her husband guessing. Husband's can be guilty of playing the same game! It's detrimental to your relationship to continue to subject your spouse to this sort of treatment. Be kind, be honest and be responsive.

Over to You!
- *Can you identify any telepathic delusions you have fallen for?*

- *Have you played a similar game of 'charades' with your spouse?*
- *Which category do you or your spouse fall into or do they respond in a different way?*
- *Are you ready to say what you mean and mean what you say?*

#marriagetip

If you forget to be open and transparent about your feelings by using 'I'm fine' type statements, don't forget you can go back and explain how you are. Explaining that you weren't honest about how you were feeling, and what the problem is, will change unhealthy communication patterns. Don't leave your spouse guessing, but say what you need to say with kindness.

Advanced Level Charades

Let's call the game of charades I just described Level One. When you enter into a cross-cultural marriage, you automatically skip to the advanced mode of the charades game. (That doesn't mean that only people in cross-cultural relationships get to play this game). This means that you really don't stand a chance of knowing what your partner is trying to communicate. Each culture has its own body language as well as its own language. While a hair flip or a foot tap or a raised eyebrow might mean one thing in your old culture, you may need a new 'sign language' dictionary in your marriage.

Many years ago, while studying in Belfast, I learned British Sign Language (BSL). I was delighted to meet deaf people when I moved to England but was rather horrified to find that my signing wasn't completely understood. Signing isn't universal, in fact, it isn't even national. Signing has its dialects too so it shouldn't be surprising that actions can have a different meaning from culture to culture. Advanced level charades requires advanced level knowledge. You need to push through and ask the difficult questions rather than just guessing at meaning.

Another form of advance level charades is when you want acknowledgement for a task that your spouse doesn't know you've performed. You might feel hurt or angry that they didn't notice all your hard work, but you don't want to tell them what you've achieved. If your spouse loved you they would notice, right? Wrong! We often assign meaning to observation skills and when your spouse's ability to show love to you is measured by that skill they might come up short.

In the early days of our marriage I dyed my hair, it was a pretty radical colour change, but Roy didn't notice. The following day I went to the hairdressers and got my hair cut. Roy still didn't notice! I stood in front of him and demanded that he tell me what he could see that was different. His eyes frantically moved around the room thinking that I had moved something, cleaned something or painted something. When he couldn't see any changes, it was obvious that he was starting to sweat. I then told him to look at me. 'What's different?' I asked again. He finally recognised I had dyed my hair but still didn't notice the haircut! If I measured Roy's love for me based on his observation skills, we would probably no longer be together. The fact is though that he does love me but observation is not the way he shows it.

Roy:
When Lainey would ask me what was different, I felt like I was being subjected to a test. From my perspective, I hated being put in that situation. I've never been good at noticing my surroundings because I'm very task focused. Lainey would often ask me in her 'teacher's voice' which made me feel even more like I was in school. I felt early on that whatever test was presented to me I would fail because there was nothing that I could do to prepare for it. I guess the correct term is 'Pop Quiz' except my answers would affect our relationship. As soon as I would realise I was being put on the spot, for another surprise test of my love for her, panic would set in. That panic made it almost impossible to think clearly no matter how much I willed myself to try. I felt as though I had been transported through time back to my school days, and those were not fun! I also had a deep sense of unfairness, it seemed (to me) that my love for Lainey wasn't measured against all of the other things I did to show my love but just this latest test.

Fortunately, Lainey wasn't as hung up about it as she could have been. It would have been easy for her to negate my other expressions of love using my lack of awareness as evidence that I didn't love her. She could have made a far bigger thing of the situation, making claims that if I really loved her I would notice these things, but she didn't. She chose to use a fairer measure to assess my love, but many people aren't that fair. They sulk, they stomp and accuse, play the hurt and offended spouse and manipulate the situation.

Now we approach life a lot differently. If Lainey does something new to the house or has been to the hairdresser, I don't have to guess what has happened. She will say something like, 'I got my hair cut today, do you like it?' Under those circumstances I am not battling with the emotions that come up; instead, I can respond naturally and take the opportunity to compliment her. I occasionally tease her when I do a job around the house or in the garden, I'll ask her, 'What's different?' Then we have a little bit of fun while she tries to discover what's new.

Over to You!

- *Have you been playing advanced level charades (either as the gamemaster or player 1)?*
- *If so, what do those games look like in your home?*
- *Have you been using the wrong measure for your spouse's love?*
- *If you were to switch roles (gamemaster/player 1) would you be uncomfortable?*

#marriagetip

It's worth taking a look at whatever you have been using as a measuring stick for your spouse's love. Ask yourself if it is fair, or if it is a measure based on Hollywood or on the measure God uses. Are there some measures you need to stop using? Don't focus on 'measuring' your spouse's performance in your marriage, instead ask yourself how you can improve in your role.

Interpretations, Assumptions and Expectations

Dr Martin Cortazzi, a linguistic expert, explains that there are three essential elements we must take into consideration when it comes to communication[8]. These three elements are interpretations, assumptions and expectations. Time and time again we have encountered situations where this has proven true in marriage.

One thing that my Roy and I learnt when we lived in Denver was the danger of assumption. Along with that, we found out that the old adage was true that the Americans and British are indeed separated by a common language.

In particular, I remember one instance when friends of ours, Joe and Stephanie DeMott, took us for a drive around Denver so we could see some of the sights. As Joe drove us into a particular neighbourhood, we were struck by what seemed to be an inconsistency. The community appeared to be affluent with beautiful homes and well-manicured lawns but on those same lawns were signs that made a different statement: 'No soliciting here!', 'No soliciting, no exceptions!', 'Absolutely no soliciting!' Roy and I exchanged confused glances, was prostitution really so out of control in the U.S.? One of us finally bit the bullet and asked Joe and Stephanie about the situation, but we were not expecting the answer they gave. The signs were to prevent door to door salesmen and had nothing to do with prostitution! British English and U.S. English were indeed worlds apart, but we had assumed we understood the signs. We think we understand each other, but in fact, there is much room for misinterpretation and misunderstanding. The difference between the way in which husbands and wives communicate

---

8   (Cortazzi, July / Sept 1996)

can be a little akin to that.

> The beginning of wisdom is this: Get wisdom.
> Though it cost all you have, get understanding.
> Proverbs 4:7 NIV

We found that Ronald L. Koteskey's explanation helped us a lot. He compares communication to an iceberg in that what you see on the surface is the smallest portion. There is a lot that lies underneath, so if you want to be accurate in your interpretations, you need to be willing to dive deep and see the bigger picture.

We want to shed a little light on what we see lies under the surface in communication between husbands and wives. Each spouse has their own frame of reference when they approach a conversation: the quality of the relationship (from their perspective), their personal culture (their upbringing), the beliefs they have (their rules or standards), their history (not only with their spouse but further into their past) and finally the hurts that they carry.

You might be wondering how to measure the quality of your relationship? While it's good to have a way to assess how your marriage is doing, in this section we want to look at how you have been measuring it. For this reason, we don't want to force our measures upon you and define it for you. For you, you may measure the quality of your relationship in terms of depth, respect, love, intimacy, friendship and trust. If you do, then these attributes are probably the things you value most. Your spouse will have different priorities and a different value system that they measure the quality of your marriage against.

Interpretation is your attempt at understanding your spouse's iceberg, not the meaning you assume because you've filtered it through your own experience. The word translation implies that you get an accurate word by word sense of the meaning your spouse is trying to convey, interpretation is not as accurate.

> "Translating from one language to another is the most delicate of intellectual exercises; compared to translation, all other puzzles, from bridge to crosswords, seem trivial and vulgar. To take a piece of Greek and put it in English without spilling a drop; what a nice skill!"
> Cyril Connolly

Most of us spill! Managing your expectations is important. While we are encouraging you both to improve in your communication skills that doesn't mean you'll suddenly have the ability to understand each other flawlessly. Whether your communication is verbal or nonverbal, it will be subject to interpretation. Both have the potential to be misunderstood, but of the two types, nonverbal (tone of voice, gesture, posture, facial expression) is perhaps the most open to misinterpretation.

Over to You!

- *Have there been any situations where you thought you understood your spouse only to find out that you misinterpreted them?*

- *Have you been translating the tip of the iceberg or the whole thing?*

- *How do you measure the quality of your relationship? (depth, quality, respect, love, intimacy, friendship and other measures)*

- *Do you understand your spouse's frame of reference?*

    - *Their relationship perspective*

    - *Their personal culture*

    - *Their history*

    - *Their hurts*

    - *Their beliefs, values, rules or standards*

- *Have you endeavoured to understand what they've been saying through that frame of reference?*

#marriagetip

It's most likely that there have been times when you have translated your spouse's words through your own framework. Spend time understanding your own framework so that you are aware of when or where misinterpretations are most likely to occur.

The Components of Communication

Since you aren't one dimensional, it makes sense to step back and consider improving communication on more than a superficial level. We have established that the human race has been created in three parts; you have been made with a body, a soul and a spirit. It's helpful when we come to look at the area of communication to tackle issues by examining those three parts. In fact, if you want to grow a successful connection, it is a huge help to explore these three aspects (body, soul and spirit) separately. It's important to remember how closely these three are interlinked.

Poor communication is one of the biggest causes of divorce, so it's vital that you learn to communicate well in all three areas since communication isn't limited to your words. You communicate in the physical sense in two main ways: with your actions and through your body language. We're also going to take a look at the three main elements of the soul: your mind, your will and your emotions. We'll examine how to convey your thoughts effectively, and learn to express feelings in a healthy way. We'll also take a look at what it means to communicate on a spiritual level, by letting God influence your communication.

Your 'body, soul and spirit' correlate closely to your words, attitudes and actions.

ACTIONS

Sofia had had enough. She was beyond frustrated with Mateo and was convinced there was no love left in their relationship. Mateo, on the other hand, expressed how much he loved his wife but believed that whatever he did was never good enough, so he'd given up trying to please her. Sofia interpreted Mateo's inaction as further proof that he had stopped caring, in her opinion there was not enough evidence to back up his declarations. To her, they were empty and meaningless.

In essence, they both knew that communication is much more complex than what they said, but they were both surprised to find out how little of their interaction was down to the words that they spoke.

According to Albert Mehrabian words only represent 7% of the message that we are delivering. His 7-38-55% Rule of Personal Communication expresses that tone of voice, and body language are also vital factors in how we relate to each other. We've found it helpful to view these categories in a slightly different way; they can be summarised as words, attitudes and actions. Since verbal communication is only one small part of the world of communication, you need to be aware that your body language, facial expressions and gestures all convey signs of how you are feeling about your spouse.

Actions Speak Louder Than Words

It is very possible to say one thing yet communicate something entirely different because of your attitude, your body language and your actions! Have you ever used the phrase, 'actions speak louder than words'?

> **Dear children, let us not love with words or speech but with actions and in truth.**
> **1 John 3:18 NIV**

In English, the word act has two meanings: 1. To do something 2. To pretend to do something. It's crucial that you put the right one in place. You have to do what you say, or what you said was worthless. Your 'body language' is not just communication through the movement of your hands or a facial expression but it is your actions that back up your words. It's how you act (as in what you do) rather than how you act (as in how good you are at pretending). The context in which this verse is used is that we should react and do something when we see someone has a need. Yet, many couples don't even do this for each other.

> 'ACTIONS SPEAK LOUDER THAN WORDS,
> AND SOMETIMES INACTION SPEAKS LOUDER THAN BOTH OF THEM.'
> MATTHEW GOOD

We hear complaints from couples all the time where one hasn't done what they said they would do. Statements like this are often accompanied with bitterness and resentment, and those emotions are not healthy in any relationship. There may be many surface-level reasons, and on the 'topical' or head level it can be true to say that there wasn't time. Being too tired, too busy or forgetful can be other valid situational factors why things weren't done. The other side of the partnership though is more likely to examine the message the inaction sent to their heart, 'the relational message'. In many cases, their interpretation is far from the intention. Your difference in priority, which causes you to think it's not something that needs to be done right now, could easily be misinterpreted as 'they don't love me.' This danger of misinterpretation is especially true if your spouse's love language[9] is Acts of Service like Sofia's.

Roy:
One bone of contention between Lainey and I was when to fill the car with diesel. I'm quite comfortable driving around on a near-empty tank of fuel as long as I can see how far I can get with the remaining fuel. Lainey, however, feels like she is driving around on fumes. She feels incredibly insecure when the levels go below a quarter full. For the longest time I refused to fill up the tank unnecessarily, in my mind her reaction was illogical, and it was a source of frustration that she overreacted. We had a few instances when the low fuel tank caused a major row between us.

Lainey felt I was insensitive to her need for security. The reality was I couldn't relate to why that would make her feel insecure, after all, we could still travel 50 kilometres before hitting the red zone on the gauge. I had to put myself in her shoes. What would it feel like for a woman on her own (in a foreign country) to be stranded without fuel? Why would she feel vulnerable in that situation? Previously I had understood her outbursts as anger towards me, but I began to realise that her dramatic response was a result of fear. Knowing this causes me to fill the tank more frequently, not because we don't have enough fuel, but rather to avoid stressing out my wife.

Occasionally I still get myself in this type of situation, mainly

---

9   If you're not familiar with love languages then we highly recommend Gary Chapman's 'The 5 Love Languages' book.

through bad planning. It is painful to see the fuel level get ever closer to zero, not because of fear of running out of fuel, but because I am now more aware of what the situation is doing to Lainey. My empathy for her grew as my understanding of her grew. Inaction can shout very loudly and send an unambiguous negative message to your spouse. You might be familiar with this phrase, "Don't talk, act. Don't say, show. Don't promise, prove.", the point of which is that you need to do something to prove your love. After all, love is a verb, and God sets the example for us to follow.

There are four things we can learn about God's character in Numbers 23:19 ESV.

"God is not man, that he should lie (1. be truthful), or a son of man, that he should change his mind (2. be consistent). Has he said, and will he not do it? (3. be reliable) Or has he spoken, and will he not fulfil it? (4. don't just start it, finish it)."

- Be truthful - if you aren't going to do something don't lie to your spouse or to yourself.

- Be consistent - building trust in a relationship takes consistency. Don't expect your spouse to focus on the one thing you did do and ignore all the other things you didn't do.

- Be reliable - do what you need to do, on time, in the right way and with the right attitude.

- Don't just start it, finish it - partly fulfilled promises can be as bad as unfulfilled promises.

Over to You!

- It's all too easy to focus on what your spouse has or hasn't done, but it's time for a self-evaluation.

- Which of these four attributes do you struggle with the most?
  - Being truthful
  - Being consistent
  - Being reliable
  - Finishing what you started

- Is your action or inaction speaking most loudly?

- Have you given up, or been tempted to give up expressing your love through actions?

#marriagetip

So often we sit back and rest on our good intentions, but we don't follow through with our actions. James 1:22 makes it clear that it is possible to deceive ourselves. 'Do not merely listen to the word, and so deceive yourselves. Do what it says.' We can fool ourselves into thinking that our spouse 'knows we love' them even though there is no physical evidence. In the 80's there was a phrase that went like this, 'If you were arrested for being a Christian would there be enough evidence to convict you?' I want to ask you a similar thing, but this time about your marriage. 'If you were charged for being in love with your spouse would there be enough evidence to support your case?' Are there specific things in your communication patterns which would make it seem like you were lying?

> 'LOVE IS A VERB, WITHOUT ACTION IT IS MERELY A WORD'.
> ANONYMOUS

The Motivation Behind Promises and Procrastination

Lainey:
Some of you could also write a book and share what the Bible has to say about relationships, you could do far better than us. However, when it comes to changing your lifestyle, you've found it difficult. You want to change, you know what you should be doing, but each time you resolve to change it lasts for a few days and then fizzles out. Roy and I have found ourselves in that situation too! If you are like us, it is something that frustrates you. It's easy to become annoyed at your own failure, it's even easier to become frustrated with your spouse when they don't get it right. You keep reading, looking for answers, hoping that something will click and a little bit like trying out the latest fad diet you are hoping for a magic pill that will make your marriage work.

We have good news, and we have bad news. The good news is that there is hope for your marriage, it can change; the bad news is that there is no magic pill. Just like having a healthy body requires discipline (eating the right food and exercising), having a healthy marriage is going to take work. You need to learn what is healthy and put it in place and you need to discard what is unhealthy. At home we have a 'treat cupboard', unfortunately, this cupboard has a tendency to lure us to it daily. When we get to a tipping point weightwise, we need to empty the treat cupboard to avoid self-sabotaging. We have to purposefully discard the things that are likely to trip us up.

We just mentioned a 'tipping point', the time and place when we realise some things need to change, and we get the motivation to do something. Roy and I have been on countless health fads over the years, but it always takes us a while to wake up and realise that our waistlines are growing and we need to do something. When it comes to your relationship, it's better when the wake-up call comes from the Holy Spirit rather than from the threat of divorce. God brings conviction when things aren't right; He brings motivation when change is needed. The difference between success and failure is listening to the voice of the Holy Spirit and being willing to change.

The parable of the two sons addresses our human tendencies, and although the context of this is regarding belief in God, there is also something we can learn about how we do life.

The Parable of the Two Sons
"What do you think? A man had two sons. And he went to the first and said, 'Son, go and work in the vineyard today.' And he answered, 'I will not,' but afterwards he changed his mind and went. And he went to the other son and said the same. And he answered, 'I go, sir,' but did not go. Which of the two did the will of his father?" They said, "The first."
Matthew 21:28-31a ESV

We don't really get insight into the emotions that either son was feeling. Were they just tired or a bit lazy or was something else going on? If you don't respond favourably to your spouse's request; examine what you are feeling. It's possible that your emotions are in the driving seat rather than the Holy Spirit. The second son exhibits some elements of passive-aggressive behaviour, stubbornness. Procrastination and failure to finish tasks can be a default response when anger has taken up residence. Passive aggressive reactions are often rooted back in childhood. If you were never taught how to express anger in a healthy way it will still find a way to manifest itself. Anger finds a more covert means to punish the offender if it's not expressed. 'I forgot', 'I didn't have time' might be true some of the time but if it's a frequent occurrence then examine your heart, has anger taken up residence?

The first son sets the example that even if we start out the wrong way, there is still time to change. When God says something, our response needs to be to act. Even if we are a little resistant at first, it is possible to change our minds and our behaviour. Laziness, for example, can be overcome. Roy and I have often found that there are days when selfishness rules our lives, we are reluctant to help each other out and would prefer to do our own thing. We see such a difference on the days when we are walking more closely with God, when we are listening and obeying Him. God highlights things that we might not even notice, and He prompts us to get up and help or simply put down what we are doing and actively listen.

Over to You!

- *Which brother do you have more in common with?*
- *Why do you think the first brother was commended more than the second brother?*
- *Can you identify any passive-aggressive tendencies in your life?*
- *Do you have difficulty expressing emotions, such as anger, in a healthy way?*

#marriagetip

Be wise about the promises you make. Ask yourself: Are they realistic? Will you have the time, energy or finances to follow through with them? Be honest, first with yourself and then with your spouse, about what you can realistically accomplish. When you promise to do something take that promise seriously and see it through.

Body Language is Both Silent and Loud

Action is an integral part of communication, but actions aren't limited to doing things, it also extends to body language. Body language provides a silent message, but one which is packed with meaning. In fact, body language can be pretty loud.

> 'The most important thing in communication is hearing what isn't said'.
> Peter Drucker

Sometimes it's not so obvious when things are unhealthy. Occasionally we find that people are amazed to discover that they are in an unhappy marriage. One man was stunned to find out that his wife was unhappy with their relationship. He had assumed that everything was going fine because his wife hadn't told him directly that there was an issue. There were warning signs, but he missed them, he hadn't understood that communication takes place on multiple levels. He was unable to 'hear' what wasn't being 'said'. Interaction is much more complicated than we assume, body language is both silent and loud at the same time.

You can learn from someone else's mistakes, don't assume that everything is going fine because your spouse hasn't said something with their lips. Read their body language too. You don't need to miss the warning signs, wake up and listen with your eyes! Although, be careful not to translate behaviour in the wrong way, if in doubt ask. Let's take busyness for example:

1. Your spouse might have way too much on their plate because they have trouble saying no to others.

2. Your spouse might be trying to fill their time because they are lonely in their relationship.

3. Your spouse might be going through a busy season and really need your help.

4. Your spouse might be upset with you and using tasks as a distraction.

Busyness is their action, but there will be other signs on their face and in the way that they move which tell you how they are feeling about what they are doing. More importantly, there will be signs which communicate how they are feeling about you.

The truth is we are always saying something, even when our mouths are closed. There is a considerable percentage shift from 7% (words only) to a whopping 55% of communication which takes place through your body language, in your face, in your stance, and in your smallest movements. Most of us don't even realise that we are picking up on cues which are non-verbal, and very few of us recognise what our own body language is telling the person we are talking to. Whatever your native language, we have access to a rich vocabulary of tens of thousands of words (remember, we use 11 million words on average per year). When we add the hundreds of thousands of micro-movements, which also express our feelings, our communication has an exponential potential to convey the depth of our hearts. Feelings like: anger, dominance, defensiveness, distress, depression, fear, attraction, deception, passive aggressiveness and power can all be expressed without saying a word.

> 'THE TONGUE SPEAKS TO THE EAR, SO THE GESTURES SPEAK TO THE EYE'.
> KING JAMES I

You don't need to go and get a degree in understanding body language, but you do need to get familiar with your spouse's reactions and what they mean by them. Roy has a habit of crossing his arms; if I went by the articles on body language, I could easily assume that he was tense or angry. While you don't need a degree to understand body language, it's dangerous to have read a short article in a magazine and imagine that you are now a body language guru. There is a lot more to it. We are certainly not experts in this area, but those who know about these things say that there are four basic rules to consider when you read someone's body language.[10]

The rule-of-four: The need for four independent yet related signals to reliably read someone's body language.

- Congruence: If what you are saying doesn't match your face or your body language then that is an incongruence which lets the other person know you aren't telling the truth or you're being sarcastic.

- Context: This is a reminder to bear in mind the setting, the timing and not building a case on one isolated incident.

- Baselining: When you know someone well (over a period of time and in a number of different circumstances), you can predict more accurately how they feel. The fact is that Roy is most comfortable when his arms are crossed, it's his 'default' setting. I know that I don't need to feel stress or worry about this posture because I know my husband. There is no need to convince him that he must be holding some unresolved anger issue, I'm at a place of peace because I know how to translate this mannerism accurately.

- Intuition and perception: This aspect can work for you, but it can also work against you. If your intuition is working well, then there isn't a problem, but if it has been damaged by past hurts, then it's likely to create an unrealistic filter. What happens when it's not working well is that we project meaning onto situations based on preconceived beliefs.

---

[10] http://bodylanguageproject.com

Roy often leans back in a chair when he is talking, that posture could easily be misinterpreted as disinterest by someone only looking for one clue to how he is feeling. The fact is that if Roy is relaxed and enjoying a conversation, he often leans back. No other aspect of his body language agrees with the assumption that he is bored or disinterested. Even if there was another indicator, it isn't enough to base an interpretation on. There should be four non-verbal indicators that show or suggest the same emotion. Some 'indicators' aren't accurate at all because they are just part of that person's personal eccentricities.

The best way to double check if you are reading someone's body language correctly is to ask them. Assuming that you are both working together to improve your communication, honesty needs to be the foundation upon which your dialogue is based. That means, avoiding saying 'I'm fine', especially if you aren't. Being willing to communicate clearly what you are feeling is vital. For the person who is reading the body language, it should also mean accepting your spouse's explanation rather than insisting you're right.

Although body language has become a science of its own, it's worth remembering that much of what we pick up about what others are thinking and feeling is instinctive. If you are struggling to interpret your spouse's mood, then you can ask them. Don't try the 'What's wrong with you?' approach, that mode of questioning will be doomed to failure. Depending on the tone with which it is said it can easily be interpreted as sarcastic, aggressive and accusative. It's better to share that you want to understand them better and you need a little help understanding what they're communicating.

Over to You!

- *Are you good at reading your spouse's body language?*

- *Do they feel you are good at understanding what they are trying to express?*

- *Are you aware of any of your own body language which could be misinterpreted?*

- *Can you identify any past hurts or 'filters' that might lead to your spouse's body language being poorly translated?*

#marriagetip

Turn your attention to your spouse when they are speaking. There will be more room for misunderstanding if you are looking at a screen (whether a phone, TV or computer) than when you look at them directly. Pay attention to what they are really saying rather than listening at surface level.

Attitudes

Your attitude may or may not be something you've thought about before when you've considered your communication, but you will undoubtedly have noticed your spouse's. The attitude behind the words you speak will carry more weight than the words alone, it also has a habit of being reflected back at you. If you start shouting it's very likely that your spouse will raise their voice too. If you are critical and bring up past offences, it should be no surprise when your spouse's historical records get dusted off and used against you. Equally, when your attitude is that of love, respect and kindness your spouse's tone will most likely soften towards you.

> Your attitude, not your aptitude, will determine your altitude.
> Zig Ziglar

Even if you are smart, articulate and have skills that would be the envy of any debate team, it's no guarantee that you know how to communicate well with your spouse. Your attitude counts.

Is it a Mouth Problem or Heart Problem?

The good person out of the good treasure of his heart produces good, and the evil person out of his evil treasure produces evil, for out of the abundance of the heart his mouth speaks.
Luke 6:45 ESV

One of mankind's most significant challenges in the area of communication is not the mouth but the heart. This verse makes it clear that what comes out of the mouth comes from the overflow (or abundance) of the heart. One thing that caught our attention was the word treasure since it seemed a bit unusual to use it in the context of the heart. Previously we had only associated 'treasure' with something good, and we wondered what evil treasure could be.

Strong's concordance defined treasure as this:
properly, stored-up treasure (riches);
(figuratively) a storehouse of treasure, including (treasured) thoughts stored up in the heart and mind.

If you treasure something, you value it. It's something you care for. If it's an object, then you might polish it or put it on display so that you can admire it. When it comes to the area of your thought life, you might not even be aware that you have put something in that position of being 'treasured'. If you go back and visit thoughts frequently, whether positive or negative, that's what is going to spill out in your conversation.

Lainey:
Most people, when they start dating, aren't thinking negative thoughts. Instead, they concentrate on the good things, the things they like. If you talk to someone who is newly in love, they can't help but talk about their loved one in gushing terms. I can remember boring everyone to tears about Roy and how wonderful he was. I treasured little things he had said and done, and he filled my thought life. Out of the overflow of my heart, my mouth spoke.

Fast forward a few years and that overflow started to change. The things I thought about were the areas in which Roy hadn't lived up to my expectations. I concentrated on the little habits which had started to irritate me, and in my mind, I built up scenarios of why. Those scenarios weren't based on truth, they were based on my imagination, and I have a good imagination! When Roy would do something else that annoyed me, I would add one more 'treasure' to the storeroom. When we would have a disagreement, I would parade all those 'treasures' before him.

When I met with my friends, we would take out all those 'treasures' and complain to each other about our spouses. Sometimes I discovered a 'treasure' I had no idea I had! Whenever I heard one of my friends talk about a lousy habit her husband had, I sometimes discovered that Roy did that too. It wasn't a bonus that I gained another thing to add to my storehouse.

Repeating an offence doesn't repair it. Forgiveness does!

God finally got my attention, and I realised that my thinking was destructive. I needed to empty the storehouse of the things that I held against Roy. The mechanism that God gives us to do that is forgiveness. If you want to improve your communication forgiveness is essential! Yet, many people find it difficult to let go of their 'treasure'.

One of my guilty pleasures in life is watching programmes about hoarding. I'm always fascinated by the fact that what many people consider to be junk or rubbish is someone else's treasure. Families intervene and try and explain the damage that hoarding is doing to the hoarder's life, their relationships and even their health and yet something compels the hoarder to hang on to their 'valuables'. Many hoarders have a fear of letting go, they can't imagine life without the things they have gathered around them. We often see couples unwilling to forgive their spouse, reluctant to let go of the 'treasure' that they have amassed even though it's doing them damage. Their mental hoarding of hurts and disappointments ruins their relationship, their family and yet they cling on to it.

Don't fear the process of forgiveness! Once the treasure room has been emptied, you can start the process of filling it with real treasure. You might wonder from where that treasure will come, this verse makes it clear.

And the peace of God, which surpasses all understanding, will guard your hearts and your minds in Christ Jesus. Finally, brothers, whatever is true, whatever is honourable, whatever is just, whatever is pure, whatever is lovely, whatever is commendable, if there is any excellence, if there is anything worthy of praise, think about these things.
Philippians 4:7-8 ESV

Over to You!

- *What type of treasure have you stored in your heart?*
- *How do you usually talk to, or talk about your spouse?*
- *Do you need to do a spring clean?*
- *Are you holding on to any 'treasure' which is damaging your relationship?*

#marriagetip

Once you've completed a 'spring clean' and forgiven your spouse, it's important to keep the treasure room of your mind clear of anything that would pollute it. If you find that your words are becoming critical, then spend time with God. Ask Him to help you stop falling into old hoarding habits.

Your Attitude is Determined by your Beliefs

Perhaps you're thinking that it is an oversimplification to suggest that hoarding negative thoughts about your spouse will have the impact we've proposed. The problem is that those negative thoughts are not fleeting, they have been rehearsed until they become a deep-seated belief. Often your attitude towards the people you communicate with is influenced by what you believe about them, their intentions towards you. Those beliefs, however, may be misguided and could be derailing your relationship.

Roy:
I have an unfortunate habit when I am communicating. Whether I'm enthusiastic or simply explaining something, I raise my voice. This tonal change Lainey misinterprets as shouting, even though in my opinion I'm merely emphasising what I want to say. The reason I do this is that in the past, amongst my school friends and later in church leadership meetings, I learned that unless I raised my voice to get my point across I wasn't heard. Ingrained ways of behaving, learnt and rehearsed behaviours, are hard to change. Even though I don't need to raise my voice with Lainey, because she listens, I still have this habit. It is proving difficult to break.

Lainey:
It's very rare that I've seen Roy angry and yet something in his tone can set me on the defensive. Why? When I've encountered loud voices in the past, they've always been because someone has been angry. Gaining deep understanding is an integral part of the process of moving towards change. That process involves looking more closely at your actions and reactions and why you behave the way that you do. Our responses are dictated by our attitudes, and our attitudes are established through our beliefs. It's been difficult for me to change my belief system. Just as $1+1=2$, my belief was that a raised voice

= anger. I have had to factor in a new equation when Roy raises his voice. A raised voice does not equal anger; it equals concern that Roy's opinion will not be heard and therefore a fear of being misunderstood.

Over the years we have sat with many couples who have been hurt by one another. Their attitude towards each other became most evident when communication revolved around a sensitive issue in their lives. Many times their verbal exchange rapidly became explosive and aggressive towards each other. Often it only took a little investigation to uncover the root cause of this. In most cases, during the conversation, a subtext was being played in the mind of the recipient. Invariably this subtext distorted the message that was intended, touched a raw nerve in the recipient, and provoked a loud and animated protective response. The source of the subtext was nearly always rooted in something that the recipient either believed about themselves or thought their spouse believed about them. Ironically the belief would never be spoken about and resulted in it remaining in place ready to cause hurt in future conversations.

To uncover unspoken beliefs requires a willingness to interrupt the exchange to get to the deeper truth. You need to clarify if your interpretation of what your spouse communicated is accurate or inaccurate. This means taking the risk of asking your spouse what they really wanted to communicate.

- Reflect. Reflection is a great skill in communication. It is the ability to listen and repeat what you heard your spouse say. Rather than interrupting with your own comeback, first give them an opportunity to complete their thought.

- Interpret. Even if you use the same vocabulary, it might mean something different to your spouse than to you. You need to act as an interpreter to help them understand what you are hearing. (This shouldn't be done in the form of an accusation, instead, assume that you are capable of misunderstanding their words and their intentions).

- Support. Deeper communication requires a high element of vulnerability. If your spouse shares with you what a word, a tone, an action or a reaction means to them don't be dismissive. Adopt a supportive stance as they share with you and avoid minimising their experiences.

- Kick-out. No! Don't kick out your spouse but rather kick out the false beliefs you've been holding on to. It can be a difficult task to let go of something you've held on to as a truth for so long, but it is necessary if you are going to be able to communicate in a healthy way.

Getting rid of false beliefs regarding your spouse will transform your attitude. When you stop allowing your emotions, that took up residence because of those false beliefs, to drive your conversations you'll find you are able to have healthy discussions. You'll be able to talk about any subject, even those which had previously been taboo topics without it ending in an argument.

Over to You!

- *What do your negative thoughts towards your spouse reveal about your beliefs?*

- *What evidence do you have to support your beliefs regarding your spouse? (Look at all the evidence, not just the evidence that supports your opinion).*

  - *Evidence for:*

  - *Evidence against:*

- *Are you basing this thought/belief on facts or feelings?*

- *Is your answer more complicated than a black or white response?*
- *Is it possible that your equation is incorrect?*

#marriagetip

Once the false belief is exposed, healing comes from allowing your spouse to dispute the belief. Follow this by taking time to look at when, and under what circumstances that belief was established within your life.

Your Beliefs can be Challenged and Your Attitude can Change

Sometimes couples find it difficult to hope for change. Past disappointment, ingrained patterns and failed attempts reinforce a sense of defeat. You don't have to settle for journeying through life in the same old ruts. It is possible to change your communication patterns. Since raised voices are such a big issue in marriage, we'll use this to illustrate the point. First, we need to take a closer look at why people yell. Psychology sheds a bit of light on this, our brain is wired to trigger the emotional centre of the brain (amygdala) when there is a perceived threat. That puts us in a fight or flight mode, a self-protective response, which often results in us yelling. Shouting or screaming isn't something you're pre-wired to do, but it is something that you learnt to do. It's possible that your spouse ends up yelling because you are screaming at them. Unfortunately, that cycle is not uncommon. It can work like this, you yell (or throw things) because you once felt threatened and learned to shout to protect yourself. Now when you hear a raised voice, you automatically feel threatened, and you quickly instigate a 'fight or flight' response.

When I was nine or ten, I was playing in our garden. My brother threw a ball to me, and in my usual awkward fashion I missed the catch and fell into a bush. Unfortunately, that meant I also crashed into a wasp's nest, and the residents of that nest weren't too happy. My reaction to the inevitable stings was to scream. That incident changed my attitude to wasps, from that point on I felt terror any time I saw one. I was so frightened of being hurt again that I couldn't bear for one to enter the house and I would automatically scream as soon as a wasp came into my line of vision. Yelling and waving my arms usually would result in another sting, reinforcing the fear and the reaction.

Many people are still caught in a cycle of behaviour because of the wounds of the past. This vicious cycle is incredibly destructive in a relationship, and any conflict usually ends up as a yelling match instead of a heart to heart. The good news is that it is possible to change, you don't need to keep responding the way you always have, it is possible to pause and think and choose a different reaction than your default one.

As an adult (still very afraid of wasps) I started teacher training. Most of the experience was in the classroom, but one of my most significant learning curves was on a class trip. We took a reception class out for the day, and everything seemed to be going well until lunch time. Everyone sat down in the picnic area and as the sandwiches were pulled out and drinks were opened it looked as though every wasp in the vicinity decided to join our picnic. I immediately felt panic rise and my fight or flight response kicked in. I received a sharp rebuke from one of the other teachers about my reaction and its effect on the children. She talked me through standing still and not reacting. I learned that not all wasps were a threat. Do you see the correlation?

The way you deal with conflict sets an example for your children. Not only can you learn that talking about problems can be non-threatening but also that it enhances your relationship, allowing you both to discuss the things that need to change and make life together better. You have an amazing opportunity to improve by applying scriptural principles rather than hiding behind old excuses such as 'that's just who I am'.

Let's take the glass half full, glass half empty 'personality types' (or perhaps you or your spouse fall into another one - 'there is no glass'). Sometimes we put these things firmly in the personality box and think they are unchangeable. While there can be a natural tendency towards one or the other, perhaps rather than being part of your personality they are a learned behaviour or response to situations.

Thinking positively or negatively has become a default setting. It is the way your brain has been wired, not by design but by a series of choices.

Have you ever found yourself in a cycle of complaint? You might think that you're communicating your needs in a healthy way, but complaining isn't communicating! In fact, complaining can drag you down a path of negativity, unhappiness and loneliness. That's because people tend to avoid those who complain because they are draining. It's important to acknowledge that each complainer has a reason for complaining. There is something they want to accomplish. If that goal isn't met, they continue to complain in the hope that the situation will change. The problem is that we get good at what we do and what we repeat.

I'm not a psychologist and would never claim to be, but I am incredibly curious about how our minds work. I read an interesting quote, "Synapses/neurons that fire together wire together" and wondered what that meant. Studies point to a brain 'rewiring' which occurs with repetitive action or repetitive thought. "Every time this electrical charge is triggered, the synapses grow closer together in order to decrease the distance the electrical charge has to cross." This reinforces the reason why many people assume that their negativity is just the way they are wired, but they don't realise they are responsible for that wiring. God makes it clear that the responsibility is ours and that it is possible to change our thought patterns.

> **Do not be conformed to this world,**
> **but be transformed**
> **by the renewal of your mind.**
> **Romans 12:2 ESV**

Time and time again God throws out challenges that feel uncomfortable and sometimes impossible.

Do everything without grumbling or arguing,
Philippians 2:14 NIV

How does that challenge sit with you? It might be easier to ignore your spouse's demands for change, but it's not so easy to push God's words aside. He is our designer, and as such He knows in which areas we are capable of change. He frequently demonstrates that what we might consider part of 'who we are' is changeable because He calls us to be more like Him.

Over to You!

- *Can you identify anything that has impacted your ability to communicate well?*

- *Which feelings are predominant in your response to your spouse?*
    - *Fear/Anxiety, Anger, Hurt, Frustration, Shame*
    - *Patience, Empathy, Secure, Calm*
    - *Other?*

- *How does that emotion influence your attitude, actions and tone of voice?*
    - *Are those responses healthy or unhealthy?*

- *If you uncover some deep issues that you are unable to deal with on your own it's important to seek help either from a counsellor or your pastor. Don't ignore the issues.*

- *Are there habits you've been excusing because you have believed it's just the way you are wired?*

#marriagetip

Self-awareness provides the platform from which you can change. What you know about yourself you can bring to God and change, what you don't know about yourself will control you. God is able to heal hurt emotions and provide you with the self-control which is needed to implement the change.

It's Not What You Say but How You Say It

On the one hand there is some truth in this saying; however, it is not the whole truth. Cruel, harsh or demeaning words will always be just that regardless of how sweetly you say them. You need to get both your attitude and your vocabulary right if you want to have a healthy relationship.

You could be using the right words, but if your tone, your body language and your actions don't back them up, then the incongruence will be evident. Your spouse will interpret your meaning by the 'loudest' expression of your communication, your attitude rather than your words. Using the wrong tone is often the reason why a husband feels disrespected even if his wife hasn't 'said' anything negative. She might say thank you for helping, but everything in her tone expresses sarcasm. The sarcasm is backed up with the body language of disgust, and hey presto disrespect is achieved even though the words could not be faulted. 'Kids say sorry to your father, he deserves your respect', could come across in two very different ways depending on the attitude and tone behind it. 'That was really clever', is an equally versatile phrase if it is said with differing tones.

Incongruence in your communication will not help you build bridges. Your words, attitudes and actions need to agree, or your communication will be skewed. That requires honesty and a mature attitude. Remember your body language is a lot louder than your speech! We've witnessed enough couples at our marriage seminars nudging each other to know how this works. We've observed many attempts at formulating a well-worded explanation only to see it fail because the delivery of those words lacked the grace that would have bridged the divide. Attitude comes across in the tone of voice you use, and that message is multiplied to the 'hearer' since it makes up 38% of communication.

The big problem with 'tone' is that our emotions drive it. Emotions not only paint a picture on your face about what is happening on the inside of you, but they also come out in your responses. If your emotions are running rampant then what you say can get pretty ugly. Even if you don't directly say something nasty, you're sending meta messages. Meta messages are like a subtext to your conversation. The phrase 'read between the lines' refers to an inferred or implied message. That message might come across in the words you choose or the questions you ask. Equally, your body language or actions can send meta messages to your spouse, and they receive an underlying meaning behind your more overt communication. Tone of voice is another vehicle for carrying meta messages. These messages can be like little love notes or, on the other hand, come across as hate mail.

It's important to examine your own behaviour and learn to express yourself in a positive manner. That means dealing with disagreements without mud-slinging. Dr Emerson Eggerichs' book Love and Respect is one we highly recommend. He talks about how vital both love and respect are in a relationship. In fact, if the opposite is present, if disrespect and lack of love are demonstrated, then relationships become dysfunctional. God did not intend relationships to disintegrate, in fact, He sets the bar high for husbands and wives.

**'However, let each one of you love his wife as himself,
and let the wife see that she respects her husband.'
Ephesians 5:33 ESV**

Unfortunately, too many people have been raised in homes where communication is unhealthy, and they haven't seen the example of love or respect. It takes work to break away from ungodly behaviours. You are not a child you are an adult, you don't have to continue the negative patterns you grew up with. As an adult, you can learn how to communicate more effectively with your spouse, not only for your own benefit but so that you can model correct communication for your kids.

You can change your legacy. Speak to your spouse with respect and don't be hypocritical in your expectations. I'm sure you've heard angry parents shout at their children for raising their voices or a frustrated spouse hurl abuse while demanding respect. If you've witnessed that you've probably been struck by the irony of the moment. Don't hold your spouse and your children to a standard that you are not willing to live by.

For some, communication hasn't grown beyond toddler tendencies. Whether you call it throwing a tantrum or having a hissy fit it still boils down to the same thing, uncontrollable emotions giving rise to unacceptable behaviour. Emotions or attitudes are not stable enough to give them the wheel of the relationship so that they can steer. When I was really young I remember going on the toddler bumper cars at the beach, I had no idea what I was doing but I turned the wheel really hard and locked it in position. The result was spinning round and round in circles until the money ran out. I stumbled out of that bumper car feeling dizzy, sick and stupid. We've seen many couples stuck, going round and round in circles unable to make progress. They don't like being trapped in a holding pattern, but they still let their emotions drive their decisions and their behaviour. If you are guilty of doing that it's time to give your emotions the sack, they're not trustworthy enough for that kind of responsibility.

Over to You!

- *What's the general tone of your communication with your spouse?*
- *Are there times when your tone worsens, e.g. when family are over, or your friends visit?*
- *Does your spouse feel loved and respected or do they believe they don't have your support?*
- *Have you allowed your emotions to drive your communication?*

#marriagetip

Respect goes hand in hand with love. Saying "I love you" without treating your spouse with respect negates the statement. If you criticise your spouse, side with the kids against them, put them down in public or belittle their input in decision-making then you need to repent. Ask God to forgive you for your attitude and ask your spouse to do the same. Start looking for the positive things, pay compliments when they do something that deserves encouragement and remember to say thank you when they do something for you.

It's Not What You Do But How You Do It

John Gottman, from The Gottman Institute, highlights four negative behaviours which are evident in unhealthy conflict. His research suggests that criticism of each other, contempt, defensiveness and stonewalling are present when a marriage is in trouble. These responses to conflict are what turns a relationship sour and makes it difficult to stomach what your spouse is trying to communicate to you. All of these behaviours reflect a heart that is in need of repair. Your attitude will seep out into your communication even if you have one aspect of your communication under control.

His recent studies indicated that certain behaviours are evident in couples heading for divorce. Eye-rolling, name calling and sarcasm were particularly damaging to relationships. While those behaviours seem to be mainly characteristic of those in the teenage years, they show up in unhealthy relationships too. There is never a justifiable reason to call your spouse names or use sarcasm, even if you think you are only being funny.

Couples might not get a hand shoved in their face, but many partners still display a teenage attitude of 'talk to the hand because this face ain't listening'. A phrase that originated in the 1990's is still alive and kicking decades later. An adult equivalent might be standing in an aggressive pose with arms folded and a defiant attitude. Why is it that adults can be as guilty as teens of dismissing what others are saying? Why is it that they don't value what their spouse is saying? Voices from their friends, wounds from the past, and confusion about the present may all play a part in their attitude and communication style. Don't let your past dictate your future.

> "Why do you look at the speck of sawdust in your brother's eye and pay no attention to the plank in your own eye?"
> Matthew 7:3 NIV

Before you analyse your spouse's behaviour deal with your own. Many couples struggle with rejection issues, and the 'talk to the hand' attitude is especially hard to deal with. The hand in the air, as a physical barrier between you and your spouse, sends a relational message 'get out of my life'. You can react to this in one of two ways.

1. Angry and upset spouses often deal with their partner's outbursts by having one of their own. They feel rejected and disrespected, and the real issue is drowned out in a row about manners. Feeling out of control often causes someone to try and control their spouse's behaviour, and that manipulation perpetuates the problem.

2. Love means that even when you are feeling rejected you still choose to love your stroppy spouse. Your love for them isn't dependent on their manners. In reality, they need you more than ever! Love suppresses the anger which would cause your reaction to be all about you, and you push through to find out what is really going on with them.

If you have been struggling as a spouse, have felt like a failure, feel like your partner is rejecting you, and have been questioning their love for you, then it's important to recognise that you have been listening to the wrong voice. It's time to tell Satan 'talk to the hand'. Reject what he has to say because Satan is a liar and he wants to steal joy from your marriage.

God formed you and is a covenant partner in your marriage. That means He knows you can do this with His help! He has chosen you, not rejected you! When you don't know what to do, what to say or how to say it, remember this advice in James.

> "If any of you lacks wisdom, let him ask God, who gives generously to all without reproach, and it will be given him. But let him ask in faith, with no doubting, for the one who doubts is like a wave of the sea that is driven and tossed by the wind."
> James 1:5-6 ESV

Over to You!

- Can you identify areas in which you need an attitude adjustment?
- Are you holding on to anger or disappointment or can you identify another emotion underlying the communication with your spouse?
- Is there evidence in your communication that your words, your attitude and your behaviour are inconsistent?
- In your relationship can you identify any of the negative behaviours John Gottman highlighted?
- What positive steps can you take to break negative cycles of contempt, criticism, defensiveness or stonewalling?

#marriagetip

Once you identify a pattern in your communication that you want to eliminate, you will become more conscious of when you fall into that cycle. You can self-correct your behaviour by changing your stance to reflect what you are really trying to say. When you realise you've done something you know has a negative impact, immediately apologise. You might recognise it immediately, half-way through a sentence or ten minutes later. Even if time has passed still apologise. Don't justify your behaviour, simply say 'I'm sorry'.

Words

We've examined the part that actions and attitudes play in communication, now it's time to look more intently at the words we use.

Words Decide Your Destination and Set Your Direction

> You have brains in your head. You have feet in your shoes. You can steer yourself in any direction you choose. You're on your own, and you know what you know. And you are the guy who'll decide where to go.
> Dr Seuss

It sounds sensible, doesn't it? You make the decisions which steer you in the direction you choose, but is that really the truth? A lot of people are willing to confess that they don't think before they speak. They don't consciously choose the words that come out of their mouths but suddenly find themselves living with the consequences of those words. Maybe you can relate to that and don't feel that your life is on the course you desired. If you want to change the direction your relationship is heading, then you need to take charge of your tongue.

James 3 is a chapter almost entirely dedicated to the words that we speak. It starts with the title 'The Taming of the Tongue'. If you've ever watched any programmes about wild animals being tamed, then you'll know that it's hard work. Every now and again a newspaper will carry a story of someone, who has worked with wild animals for years, being mauled by a 'tamed' beast. Some of you will have had the unfortunate experience of being under attack from your partner's tongue. However, many of you will have been the one who has lost control.

> For we all stumble in many ways. And if anyone does not stumble in what he says, he is a perfect man, able also to bridle his whole body. If we put bits into the mouths of horses so that they obey us, we guide their whole bodies as well.
> James 3:2-3 ESV

I didn't know a lot about horses and horse riding, but I wanted to understand how the bridle works to guide a horse. I did a little research so I could understand what they were and what they did. A lot of bridles have something called a 'bit', which goes into the horse's mouth. It puts pressure on the back of the mouth but also on the tongue of the horse. In other words, the bridle is designed to give the rider control rather than the horse.

That one little piece of your body, your tongue, can steer the direction of your life. No one wants to steer their lives in the wrong direction; however, the rash words that can come out of your mouth sets your course. It's important to recognise that it isn't a small muscle in your mouth that's the main problem, the tongue is activated by your mind, your will and your emotions. In other words, it's usually operated out of the soul area. That's what gets people into difficulty!

Sandra frequently made threats of going back to her mother or divorcing Tom. She had a fiery temper and when she got angry words would tumble out that she couldn't take back. After one particularly strong tirade, Tom had had enough. He took her at her word when she asked him, 'Why don't you just pack your bags and leave?' She had inadvertently been steering her marriage by her words.

> **Look at the ships also:**
> though they are so large and are driven by strong winds,
> they are guided by a very small rudder
> wherever the will of the pilot directs.

James 3:4 ESV

Tom slowly unpacked his bags as Sandra sobbed her heartfelt apology. They both knew that for this to work something had to change in their language. Are you willing to change yours?

If you are guilty of using your words unwisely, then you need to recognise that what you aimlessly say still sets a direction for your life. James chapter 3 goes on to press home the point by using another analogy. James compares the damage the tongue can do to the devastation of a forest fire, which is caused by something tiny. Forest fires aren't usually started deliberately, a discarded cigarette butt or a BBQ gone wrong can destroy thousands of acres of land very quickly. James warns that what we say impacts others, not just us, and sets 'on fire the entire course of life'. You've probably already noticed some things that you say that sets your spouse off, perhaps you've dismissed it as their problem. It might be worth examining your words in case you're causing the spark.

Over to You!

- *Is your marriage on a crash course because you've been allowing your words to steer you in the wrong direction?*
    - *Are you willing to let the Holy Spirit steer rather than your mind, your will and your emotions?*
- *Do you ever threaten to leave home or divorce?*
    - *Be careful not to repeat those threats, they undermine your relationship and set you on the wrong course.*
- *Can you identify anything your spouse says or does which causes a negative reaction within you?*
- *Can you identify anything you say or do that causes an adverse reaction in your spouse?*

#marriagetip

When you identify a trigger or something that causes your emotions to take control of your tongue, there are a few things you can do. Ask yourself these questions: What emotion do I feel right now? How long have I felt this way? (Often triggers are rooted in the distant past). Do I want this emotion to set my destination? Usually, the answer will be 'NO!' If your feelings have been in the pilot seat, pausing long enough to process will enable you to press the eject button on your emotions and put the Holy Spirit back in control.

What to Say and What not to Say

In this terrain, there are dangerous landmines that lurk under the surface of what can seem like perfectly innocent conversations. Some of these landmines will erupt and take out personnel (namely you), others have the potential to take out a tank. They include cultural mindsets, politics, religion and unknown taboos.

> **Don't talk so much. You keep putting your foot in your mouth.
> Be sensible and turn off the flow!
> Proverbs 10:19 TLB**

Keeping in mind that you are learning culture rather than just learning language will help you with discovering what you should and shouldn't say in different situations. Our daughter Beth suffered from a particularly bad case of 'foot and mouth' disease when we first moved to Denver, Colorado. Beth's first day at school could not be described as the best day of her life. She encountered a world for which she had no cultural reference and which felt like she had landed on another planet. In this alien land, she was probed by many questions relating to where she had come from and what she thought of America. Already feeling overwhelmed the bell rang to indicate the start of her first school day.

Beth looked around the classroom as everyone stood to attention and placed their hands on their hearts. Beth followed suit and stood placing her hand on her heart too. All her classmates knew the drill and dutifully recited the Pledge of Allegiance. 'I pledge allegiance to the Flag of the United States of America, and to the Republic for which it stands, one Nation under God, indivisible, with liberty and justice for all.' Beth not only did not know the Pledge of Allegiance but it was a bridge too far to give up her 'Britishness'.

At break-time (recess) she was surrounded by a group of rather annoyed school kids who demanded to know why she didn't know the Pledge of Allegiance. Beth's response was to ask if they knew the British National Anthem. That seemed like a fair question to Beth, but it seemed to throw fuel on the fire. Beth now exasperated by the conversation made the following statement and in doing so delayed making friends for a few months, "Hello! America is not the centre of the universe!" This was evidently not the right thing to say in that circumstance.

Sometimes you won't know that you have stepped on someone's toes until they scream. Communication is like that, it is hard to anticipate every difficulty and avoid it. It is important though when you do make a faux pas that you learn from it. Don't just mumble an apology and plead ignorance, make sure that your apology is genuine.

There are some destructive habits which we've seen time and time again which you can avoid. In the following paragraphs, we're going to take a look at some of these. Hopefully, they will help you avoid some of the pitfalls, or make some much-needed changes, to the way you relate to your spouse.

One thing we often see are generalisations used to accuse, justify or fuel a dispute. Our advice is to avoid using language which includes extremes like always and never. Things like, 'You never help around here' will come across as unfair when your spouse does other things around the home. If you're guilty of doing this, it's possible you are focusing in on one flaw and are blind to the good that your spouse does. 'I always have to do everything' is another expression of the same extremes. When you find yourself using words like always, never, everyone, every time and everything then challenge that thought. Is it true or can you see evidence that there are circumstances when it is not accurate? Instead, try using words like sometimes, occasionally, rarely, words that more accurately reflect the actual situation.

Another destructive habit to avoid is to tackle a huge list of things that might not be going well in your relationship. This usually results in your spouse feeling overwhelmed and discouraged. You might wonder which topic to choose, especially if you do have a giant list. Sometimes it is best to start small with something that is easily sorted out rather than diving straight in and dealing with the biggest issue. It really depends on how healthy or unhealthy your communication has been in the past. If it has been volatile, then 'practice' by addressing a less heated subject. Stick to the targeted topic, no digressions, no distractions and no additions (even if you've covered a topic and it went pretty well). As a general rule of thumb, a relationship needs to have many more positives than negatives to be healthy (the ratio is 5:1). If your conversations are filled with negativity and complaint, then you are missing an opportunity to build your relationship.

Talking 'at' one another instead of 'to' one another is another destructive habit that needs to be challenged. Don't go into lecture mode, rather let the conversation flow. Listen to what your spouse has to contribute. If you have a habit of talking 'at' one another, try and understand why you have that pattern. Is it something that was modelled to you? If that's the case, then remember your template for healthy communication should come from God's word. Try this instead:

Know this, my beloved brothers: let every person be quick to hear, slow to speak, slow to anger.
James 1:19 ESV

There are things we should do quickly and things we should do slowly. In the area of communication, most people are the opposite, they are slow to hear, quick to speak and quick to anger. They are also quick to jump to conclusions. That's because we make, or create, meaning from or associate meaning with certain words or actions. It's easy to assume that your spouse 'forgot' to do something deliberately. It's possible that your conclusion isn't the truth. They may have had other stressful things on their mind which took priority or caused them to forget. Quick assumptions lead to quick anger, which leads to quick words. Slow down, intentionally make hearing and understanding your primary goals.

Over to You!

- *Can you recognise any patterns that need to change in your communication?*
- *Which one can you relate to the most?*
- *Is there another communication pattern which you know you need to avoid?*
- *Which one will be the most challenging?*
  - *What do you intend to put into place to help correct that pattern?*

#marriagetip

If you find your spouse reacting negatively to something you say, ask yourself if there is a better way to communicate that thought. Try and resist the temptation to accuse your spouse, belittle them or hurl insults. If your spouse is hurting they aren't hearing, they will 'go deaf' to what you are trying to say.

Pillow Talk

Pillow talk refers to conversations between a husband and wife which they don't share with the world. They are more intimate and private in nature but also are affirming and appreciative. Although there are plenty of day time opportunities to use words to love, cherish, appreciate and affirm your spouse it often doesn't happen enough. Some people find it more difficult than others, not necessarily because they don't love their spouse, simply because it hasn't been modelled to them. You may be thinking positively about your partner, but it is important to share that with them. Tell them that they look nice, compliment them on their achievements, thank them when they do something (even if you think it shouldn't need thanks because it's just part of their role). Appreciation is recognising the full worth of your spouse. If your spouse has ever accused you of not appreciating them, then you've probably not been using words of affirmation enough.

When you were dating, you may have found it easier to pay your spouse complements. In marriage, those compliments are just as important. Words play a large part in ensuring your spouse feels cherished and treasured. If your words have been used to make them feel disrespected, undervalued or of no worth, then it's time to make a change. It might feel a little awkward to change the way in which you communicate, but it will be well worth the effort.

Because this section is called pillow talk, you might have been expecting that this section is only going to dive into the area of whispering sweet nothings to each other, but now we want to focus instead on the type of 'pillow talk' that's destructive. Some couples think that bedtime is a good time to bring up all the problems, stressors and disagreements of the day. The principle, 'Don't let the sun go down on your anger' is quoted to justify such nocturnal communication, but is it really healthy? For years, Roy and I lived under the illusion that we had to get any and every disagreement sorted out immediately. If we had any issue that wasn't resolved, we incorrectly thought we needed to invest time in getting it fixed ASAP. Many times we went to our bedroom only to enter a war room. Bedtime (yes, the time when we were both at our worst when our energy had gone when we were tired and cranky) became the time when we would try and sort out any 'unfinished business'. The result for us was often a half-hearted truce at best, at worst it involved us lying as far away from each other as possible almost clinging to the side of the bed in case we fell out.

We had been taught, 'Don't let the sun go down on your anger', and we were doing our best to put it into action, but something wasn't working. We went back to the verse and were surprised to discover its context, what it actually said, and more importantly what it meant for us.

In context, Ephesians 4 is a chapter which encourages love and unity and living a life of spiritual maturity. The second half of the chapter focuses on what it is like to live in that new life and the changes that need to be made. Much of that involves removing the things that are part of the old life and embracing a new way of relating to one another. Verse 25 sets the challenge to become honest with one another. Then we get to verse 26 where we find the famous line 'Do not let the sun go down on your anger', but let's look at it a little more fully.

The full verse:

Be angry and do not sin;
do not let the sun go down on your anger.
Ephesians 4:26 ESV

The Amplified Version puts it this way:

> **Be angry [at sin—at immorality, at injustice, at ungodly behaviour], yet do not sin; do not let your anger [cause you shame, nor allow it to] last until the sun goes down.**

Some translations say 'Don't let your anger lead you into sin' or 'Don't let your anger control you'.

As we read this together, we got a bigger picture of what this verse meant and especially how to apply it to us as a couple. For us, this was no longer a second-hand principle, it wasn't something that had been misinterpreted which we were struggling to implement. It was no longer something that we blindly followed because someone had taught on it. There is no hint that this verse is advocating fully resolving conflict before you go to sleep. Instead, it focuses on the emotions behind the conflict, the thing that can cause hate or bitterness to grow in your relationship. Winning an argument isn't the goal, so turning your bedroom into a battlefield before you go to sleep isn't the aim. The aim is to sleep in peace because your mind is at rest without the emotional baggage of the day.

There are a few things we can draw from this. Firstly, we have a responsibility not to fall into the trap of sinning while we're annoyed at injustices or immorality that we see around us. Don't let those emotions develop into something that damages relationships or seeks vengeance. The focus isn't on what others have done, it isn't on convincing them of our way of thinking, it's about dealing with our personal emotions quickly. Those who have a tendency to forgive slowly or huff, need to take this on-board especially.

Secondly, we have power over our anger, it should not control us. If there is a battle in the bedroom, it should not be a struggle of wills between a couple. It should instead be fighting a spiritual battle in prayer. The spiritual battle should be asking for God's help to win a personal battle, the battle over the tendency to keep hold of anger and do or say something sinful because of that anger.

The next principle we see is that we need to learn to deal with our anger quickly and not let it continue to eat away at us until the next day. The urgency is to deal with our attitude, that doesn't mean never talking about issues, it simply means finding a sensible time to talk! Let's zoom out a little more and read the principle in its broader context.

> **"In your anger do not sin": Do not let the sun go down while you are still angry, and do not give the devil a foothold... Do not let any unwholesome talk come out of your mouths, but only what is helpful for building others up according to their needs, that it may benefit those who listen. And do not grieve the Holy Spirit of God, with whom you were sealed for the day of redemption. Get rid of all bitterness, rage and anger, brawling and slander, along with every form of malice.**
> **Ephesians 4:26-27, 29-31 NIV**

The next verse (verse 27) warns that anger can give a foothold to the enemy. It's essential that as a couple you don't let Satan have a single piece of ground in your home, and yet many of us have invited him into the most intimate place in our homes. Your bedroom is a place where your focus should be on your spouse, a place of love and intimacy. The privacy of your bedroom shouldn't be invaded by the sounds of battle, a place you associate with arguments. So what do you do when you disagree?

There is a lot more that we can learn from Ephesians as we continue to explore this verse in its context.

1. We don't need to sin just because we felt angry.

2. We shouldn't leave the anger unresolved because it gives the devil

a foothold.

3. We need to be careful what we say, especially in moments of anger.

4. Build others up and don't grieve the Holy Spirit.

5. Get rid of the negative behaviours such as 'bitterness, rage and anger, brawling and slander along with every form of malice.'

While these are universal principles for Christian lives and relationships, it is especially important that it is something that you practice in your own home. Your home should never be a place where physical, emotional or spiritual abuse takes place. The only person you can change is you. Personal change is the only thing you can control; you cannot control the action or inaction of your spouse. Your husband or wife has to do their own changing. You can pray for them: but don't nag them. Nagging is always counterproductive in the long term.

> "YOU CAN BE RIGHT BUT WRONG AT THE TOP OF YOUR VOICE"
> EMERSON EGGERICHS[11]

Over to You!

- *Have your words been demonstrating your appreciation of your spouse?*

    - *If you feel you could do better, can you identify opportunities that you've been missing?*

- *When do you generally talk about issues that you have between you?*

- *Has your bedroom been an oasis or a battlefield?*

- *What do you feel that God is asking you to do in response to these verses?*

---

11   Love & Respect: The Love She Most Desires; The Respect He Desperately Needs

#marriagetip

Deal with your anger. Roy and I know that our hearts are for each other, even on the days when we don't agree. If we are going to get angry with anyone we try to make sure it is channelled in the right direction - at the enemy who wants to steal, kill and destroy.

Agree when you are going to resolve any issues between you. It would be very easy for someone who has an aversion to conflict to use this as an excuse to never deal with issues. If it's late when we have a disagreement, we decide when would be the best time to talk about what is happening between us. This doesn't allow problems to be swept under the carpet but does allow us to get enough sleep so we can do life the next day.

Reaffirm your love for each other. We take the opportunity to reassure each other of our love, that we do care, that we want to solve the issues and we will work towards that.

Pray together. We pray that God will help us in the battle with our emotions and that He will give us wisdom in solving any problems between us.

A hug or cuddle doesn't go amiss either!

You can't Nag and Whine your Way to a Better Marriage

Nagging is a habit which is an unfortunate feature of too many marriages. Nagging is not just unhealthy; it's harmful. There is a big problem though, it isn't that easy to stop! Roy has a few favourite verses which he loved to quote to me when I would fall into the pattern of nagging. We aren't recommending this approach since it didn't work out very well for us. His first choice was usually,

> 'It is better to live on a corner of a roof
> than to share a house with a nagging wife'.
> Proverbs 21:9 NIRV

This verse really says it all, when either of you nags your spouse, you're more likely to encourage them to move out than to do what you want them to do. That's probably why so many men have migrated to the garden shed or to the garage. Part of the problem though is that nagging isn't one-sided, there are two people in the relationship who perpetuate the nagging cycle.

So, when does a request become nagging? There is a fine line separating a request for help from nagging territory. That fine line makes it difficult for many to identify what they are doing. It's okay to ask for some help. We don't want you to get the wrong impression and think that you have to suddenly start wearing a leotard and cape, you aren't superhuman! It's not inconsiderate to expect others in your home to pull their weight. It is important though to know how to ask and get results. A request becomes nagging when it is repeated again and again, often with an accompanying negative tone. If you start hearing yourself sounding like a broken record, then something is broken in the area of communication. It's also important to think about the tone of your request. It might have started off on the right level, but after having to repeat it several times, the tone usually becomes less than healthy.

For some, nagging is a natural progression from the whining of childhood. They found as a child that repeating themselves again and again until their parents caved in produced results. They wore down 'the opposition' in the hope that they would get what they wanted. They then take the same strategy and apply it to their adult role, whether it be as a spouse or as a parent.

Roy's second favourite quotable 'nagging' verse was also in Proverbs.

> **The steady dripping of rain and the nagging of a wife**
> **are one and the same.**
> **Proverbs 27:15 CEV**

Most people would agree that a child whining is pretty annoying, it certainly grates on my nerves! Yet, most people who nag have no idea how irritating they have become. They focus on the object of their nagging, rather than their own behaviour, and often lose sight of the part they play in this negative cycle. The steady dripping of rain reminded Roy of Chinese water torture, and although that might get you results, it's most likely that the victim will want to escape as soon as possible rather than express their love for you.

On the other side of the nagging cycle is the non-compliant spouse. This husband or wife refuses to respond to their spouse's requests no matter how reasonable. It seems as though they have an automatic 'dig-in-their-heels' response to any and every request. The non-compliant spouse feels justified in not 'giving in' to their spouse. They may even start to see their partner as bossy and overbearing because the nagging is getting on their nerves. They simply start to tune them out. This response often has its roots in childhood too. As a child, this spouse learned that if they could ignore their parents' requests, zone them out, be stubborn and resistant, they could get away without doing their part in the home.

Men tend to be more non-compliant than women because they view obeying a request as an acknowledgement of hierarchy.[12] The power play involved in both nagging and non-compliance needs to be understood but not used as an excuse. Both husbands and wives need to own the fact that their behaviour perpetuates the situation. Here's how it goes. The wife asks the husband to help clear up after the evening meal, she feels it's a reasonable request since she cooked. He hears the request as a command and decides not to jump up in obedience, so he delays his response. The wife returns to the kitchen and discovers that no progress has been made, she feels hurt and uncared for because he hasn't shown willingness to help. Again, she attempts to broach the subject, after all, there must be a reasonable explanation, he must have gotten distracted or forgotten. The husband hears the second request which to him is a power play, he must now resist at all costs. He will do the job later, in his time, in his way, then he will be back at the helm. The more requests he receives, the more he digs in his heels. He accuses his wife of being a nag, and she accuses him of being lazy. They've both contributed to the stress.

> "BOTH NAGGING AND BEING RESISTANT ARE CHILDISH BEHAVIOURS
> WHICH DESTROY AN ADULT RELATIONSHIP!"

Over to You!

If either of these responses resonates with you, then you have bad habits to break. If you both own the problem, then you are more likely to see results.

---

12 Tannen Deborah: You Just Don't Understand Women and Men in Conversation

This means that you are going to need to sit down and have an honest conversation, and that starts off with being honest with yourself.

- *Are you making unreasonable requests? What might seem reasonable to you, might seem over-the-top to your spouse. If you are verging on OCD, don't force your spouse to keep those standards. You should be able to expect help, but make sure that 'help' is not slavery.*

- *Have you been hurling insults as well as nagging? Too often in desperation, people take to saying hurtful things hoping that it will spur their spouse into action. If you are guilty of this, you couldn't be more wrong! Tell your spouse that you are sorry, make sure you offer them a sincere apology.*

- *Are you resisting reasonable requests? Perhaps you have been digging in your heels when you should be getting up to help. If this sounds like you, ask your spouse to forgive you. It's almost inevitable in this type of relationship there will be resentments on both sides, so it's also necessary for you to forgive them too.*

- *Have you become defensive in your response? If you find that you are always justifying your actions or inactions take the time to see if that defensiveness is warranted. Are there areas in which you should step up to the plate?*

- *Have you given up because you never seem to be able to please your spouse? This is a problem you both need to work through. It means taking action and doing your part, but it also means your spouse needs to lay down criticism and start appreciating your contribution.*

#marriagetip

We have found the following verse a helpful guide when we have needed an attitude readjustment. Why not stick it to the fridge as a reminder to break the nagging cycle.

**Do nothing from selfish ambition or conceit,
but in humility count others more significant than yourselves.
Philippians 2:3 ESV**

Silence
Learning to Shut Your Mouth

'Shut it', 'shut up' and 'shut your mouth', are phrases that are used to get someone to stop talking, but they're often considered rude. It's an abrupt way to interrupt, and most people consider it to be disrespectful. I'm not advocating that we start using the phrase but perhaps you might need to examine what you've been saying and how you've been saying it. It's important to take notice and realise that there are times when you do need to be quiet because words can be damaging.

You might feel offended by what I've just said but I've learned the hard way that there are times when 'Silence is Golden'. I love to talk, maybe because I didn't speak until the age of three, and my mum says that I've been trying to make up for that ever since. Since then I've been trying to catch up on 33 million words! I used to feel very uncomfortable with silence and thought it was my job to step in and fill it, even if it was a lot of stuff about nothing, it seemed better, less awkward. Over the years I've realised that it's often not wise. There's a little saying, 'Lord fill my mouth with worthwhile stuff and nudge me when I've said enough'. This became a prayer for me, I wanted my words to be directed by Him not me.

Perhaps, like me you are a talker and silence makes you uncomfortable. If that's the case, it can drive you into a monologuing frenzy. You might consider a monologue to be valid communication, but it is one way, unengaging and comes across as though you don't care about anyone else's opinion. Put yourself in your spouse's shoes, I'm sure that you've spent time with someone who likes the sound of their own voice and never seems to come up for air. They can speak for 10, 15, or 20 minutes and no one can get a word in edgeways. Having a conversation with them is impossible. They are the sort of people that you try to interrupt but fail, or you simply can't find a big enough break to jump in. Do you do the same to your spouse?

> "CONVERSATIONS BETWEEN TWO PARTIES
> WHO ARE NOT REALLY LISTENING TO EACH OTHER
> ARE ESSENTIALLY MONOLOGUES MASQUERADING AS DIALOGUES".
> KIM SCHNEIDERMAN L.C.S.W., M.S.W

We don't intend to go into all the reasons why people resort to monologuing; however, one of the primary reasons is that they usually have an agenda. Something important to them that they wish to communicate, essentially they want to be heard. The problem is that if the thing they want to express is elevated to a higher importance than the thoughts and feelings of the listener, it becomes detrimental to the relationship. Learning to stop monologuing, to give time and space for your spouse to share their thoughts and feelings is essential for a healthy conversation. True love can sound like silence, the willingness to be still and listen.

The same can be said for the times we spend time with God. Are you monologuing? Do you come to Him with an agenda, perhaps even with some suggestions of how He could fix things? One of the best places to learn being still, being quiet and listening is in the presence of God. True love is also letting the Holy Spirit speak to your hearts about what God wants for your life.

Over to You!

- *Are you prone to talk too much or too little?*
- *Do you find it easy to interrupt the flow of conversation with your own opinion? (Not in a rude way, but you are able to jump in when there is a natural gap).*

- *Do you allow others to interrupt your flow of conversation? (Do you pause and give room for others to contribute?)*

- *Is your communication with your spouse your monologue, a dialogue or their monologue?*

- *In your conversations with God is it one-way or two-way communication?*

#marriagetip

Imagine that every time you speak, you are holding a microphone. There is only one microphone in the room, and your spouse doesn't get to talk unless you stop. Are you hogging the mic, refusing to take the mic or do you have equal microphone time?

When to Speak and When to be Quiet

... A TIME TO BE SILENT AND A TIME TO SPEAK
ECCLESIASTES 3:7 NIV

There is a lot of wisdom packed into this verse. Did you know that there are cultural differences regarding when it is acceptable to talk and when it isn't? The answer becomes very obvious as soon as you start contemplating the question through the filter of the stereotypes we have of different nations. If you consider a nation to be noisy or another to be exceptionally quiet, then it becomes evident that there is a 'when to talk' rule in place. The same cultural principle applies to couples who have grown up in the same nation or even in the same locality. Some households are loud, and some are quiet, each home has its own unspoken communication rules.

A negative stereotype of a family culture usually develops because one family judges the other family on what they do that differs from their own. Those negative stereotypes can become ingrained, and you can end up judging your spouse unfairly because of that filter. A family culture that is perceived to be too loud may be misjudged as being insensitive, insincere, overbearing and obnoxious. A family culture that is perceived to be too quiet may be misjudged as being sullen, sulky, uncooperative or even stupid.

It's important to apply the knowledge, understanding and wisdom principle. Ask yourself the following questions:

- What do you know about 'when to talk' in your spouse's home culture?

- How comfortable is his/her family with silence?

- When you visit your spouse's family what is their home environment like?

- Do you find the family too talkative or too quiet?

When you have answered those questions, you have some knowledge. Now it is crucial to press through to the next level, to a place of understanding. Discovering why people are the way that they are is much more difficult. It involves asking a different type of question, one that doesn't tap into the facts but taps into the feelings. For example:

- How do you feel when people are silent?

- What do you think that silence means?

Silence is still communicating. For you it might mean peace, calm and contentment but what is it communicating to your spouse? In my childhood home, silence was extremely rare. Silence could mean a number of things, but most meanings were negative. Silence could be because someone was upset and didn't want to talk. Silence could also be because I had done something wrong. Silence was always uncomfortable for me, and I would make every effort to fill it. I didn't even like silence when I was alone. Now silence means something very different to me. I like silence; I love the peace and quiet when the only noises I hear are birds in the trees. I find silence relaxing and am comfortable sitting with my husband without the need to 'fill' what I used to believe was an empty space. My perception of silence changed as a result of my relationship with Roy who came from a completely different background.

Of course, you can ask questions regarding the other extreme too:

- How do you feel when people are talkative?

- What do you think that characteristic says about them?

We can be so predisposed to judge someone, not just on what they say but the amount they say. Stepping into some cultures can feel like stepping into a car showroom where an overzealous salesperson is waiting. You can feel swamped by an over stimulus of information and filled with concern that if you don't find the exit quickly, you will be sold something or persuaded to take a test drive. Rather than receiving the welcome as friendly, it can be perceived as deceptive and conniving.

Wisdom understands that different is just different, it's not wrong. Rather than arguing about which style is best you both need to move towards finding a noise level that works for you both and the right rhythm for your communication with your spouse.

Pacing and pausing is a term used regarding the speed of speech and those natural little pauses which allow someone else to participate in the conversation. If those are a bit off-beat when you communicate with your spouse, your conversation might resemble my attempts at using a skipping rope. You know the type of skipping where someone stands at either end of a long rope slowly turning it and probably chanting a silly song. There is a rhythm, and you need to get the timing right so that you can jump in and start skipping. The rope continues to turn, and you are supposed to jump and count as it rotates. It doesn't go like that for me. I watch the rope and try to find the rhythm, I psych myself up to jump in and finally make the big leap only to find that I have horribly misjudged it. I remember that feeling of failure and deflation hitting me at the same time as I felt the rope hitting off my legs before even making one jump. I feel a little like that if I'm talking to someone and the conversation isn't flowing well.

If your conversation style is different than your spouse's, it can create a foreign rhythm which results in the pacing and pausing part of conversations becoming awkward. Even if a husband and wife have managed to work out their timing between them, they can find family parties a strain. This is often where the differences in conversation styles become most apparent. Have you ever noticed your spouse glaring at you from the other side of the room and you don't have a clue what you have done to cause an upset? It may be that you haven't been aware of the conversation cues around you that are so evident to your spouse.

You might imagine that after thirty years of marriage Roy and I have become masters at this pacing and pausing game. You assume wrong. Sometimes I misjudge Roy and think he has nothing to say or add to a conversation when he simply hasn't been given the opportunity. Roy on the other hand sometimes misjudges me and feels like I don't want to give him a chance to be heard.

Knowing that pacing and pausing is important in a conversation is something that can switch a light on in a relationship. It reveals that there may be a reason beyond what we see on the surface as 'rude' behaviour. Understanding that each person, having their own unique culture, has their own rhythm of conversation can really help us push judgement to the side. The question is though - how do you both get in rhythm with each other? As you start to learn how to establish a good rhythm in your conversation, there are times when you will get it wrong. That's fine, it isn't something to worry about, just make an effort to keep on working at it and learn to laugh when you miss-time a jump, and you crash into the rope. It will be fun when you get the hang of it!

Tension can arise in a relationship when you overstep your spouse's boundary and break their 'when to speak' rule. For those who are comfortable with silence, having a spouse who fills every quiet moment can be problematic. This is where you need to move from knowledge to understanding and finally to wisdom.

We have seen a substantial cultural contrast especially with dear friends of ours. Timo and Yolanda are a Finnish/American cross-cultural couple. Timo is no ordinary Finn though, he is an extrovert and breaks the Finnish stereotype by being unusually chatty. With that having been established, Timo is also very comfortable with silence. He does not feel uncomfortable if someone asks him a question and he contemplates it for quite a while before choosing to answer. Yoli has had to develop wisdom over the years and ignore her desire to step in and respond on his behalf. She understands that his slowness to answer is deliberate and not an inability to understand, nor is it in any way a reflection of his ability to share his thoughts. In fact, they have a great deal of respect for one another, and an acceptance of their differences. They simply have different social rules about when to talk, and they give each other grace in their differences.

What can you do with all that information? In previous books, we've hammered home the principle that different is just different; it's not wrong. Approaching your spouse's communication style as wrong will only irritate them. However, if you grow in understanding each other, you'll find that your communication style will start to adjust. When we were first married we were at opposite extremes, now Roy is much more talkative than he used to be and I am much quieter. We are not the same and being identical is not our goal. Our aim is to leave room for each other. I need to be quiet, so Roy can have space to think and formulate a response, while Roy needs to speak so I know he is engaged in the conversation and so that I can hear his heart.

Over to You!

- *What is the rhythm of your communication like? (natural/unnatural)*
- *Do you have a tendency to jump in and finish your spouse's sentences?*

- Are you both happy about that or does it irritate one of you?
* What do you know about the 'when to speak' rules your spouse has?
  - Do they differ from your own?
  - If you need to find common ground how are you going to accomplish that?

#marriagetip

There are lots of other rules regarding when to speak that we haven't explored here. Whether meal times are noisy or silent, whether it's okay to speak when the TV is on, whether it's okay to have a conversation the moment you come home from work or if you need fifteen minutes to relax and clear your head. When you identify a personal 'rule' share it with your spouse and try and understand what their rule is. Together you can decide your family's culture.

When to Say Nothing

There are times when it is wise to say nothing at all. Those will vary from couple to couple and person to person, but there are some general principles which we have found to be true for most couples. Are they true for you?

It's best to say nothing when your spouse hasn't asked for your advice. Here is an account of how this went wrong for Lainey and I.

Sweat oozing from every pore upon my brow, muscles straining as I fought, determined to strengthen my vice-like-grip on the screwdriver, I engaged in a battle of wills. It was me versus a stubborn screw. The struggle was real, and if I was to successfully tile the wall in front of me I had to win, the screw had to lose, this sucker was going down. Except it wasn't! No matter how hard I tried, the screw remained, a defiant obstacle to progress. It was about then that Lainey innocently suggested that I tried a different approach. My response was not kind.

I know we are all unique, not carbon copies of one another, but we all regularly identify with things that stereotypically describe traits of either our gender, our stage in life or our Myers-Briggs personality profile. The important thing is to realise these observations often ring true, but they don't define us or the way we behave. They are just useful in allowing us to understand something about whatever portion of the population we are looking at. Neither should we be concerned if we don't fit the stereotype.

With this in mind, stereotypically men do not respond well to unsolicited advice. If a man needs help or advice, he will ask for it. Actually, he probably won't if he follows other traits typical of men. For example, men usually resist asking for directions even when they are hopelessly lost. This stereotype is particularly true of me.

The example above is an extreme one, but it does emphasise the need to respect each other's boundaries. I know I've fallen into that trap when I've given unsolicited advice about something Lainey is doing whether it's cooking, writing or painting. We can, and probably do hold an opinion about most things we see or hear, and we have a right to that opinion. We do not, however, have a right to barge into some element of someone's life and meddle. Nor should we discount, deride or control our spouse by forcing our opinion upon them. Rather than giving your opinion, wait to be asked. If you really believe your advice would help, then ask first if they want your opinion or simply ask questions that check understanding and help them to see a different perspective.

Since we are looking at stereotypes, men invalidate feelings and provide solutions. This also is very true for me. Typically, when Lainey starts describing how she is feeling, or what is happening in her life my mind searches for solutions. I jump in, part-way through, telling her either what she did wrong or what she needs to do to fix the situation. Maybe it is the engineer in me, or perhaps it is the man, that causes me to naturally do this.

However natural this is for me, it is still often the wrong response. It sends so many incorrect messages. Firstly, it makes the assumption that Lainey doesn't know how to change the situation. It carries a relational message that only I can fix Lainey's problem. The sub-text states that I believe she is incapable of doing the right thing. Secondly, although my desire to fix the situation demonstrates, in my thinking, that I care for Lainey - it actually does the opposite. In her interpretation, it demonstrates that I am uncaring and not concerned about how she feels.

In these situations, I have learned, that what Lainey needs is to be heard not taught, listened to not talked at. For me, it takes superhuman effort not to offer solutions and to listen instead, to empathise rather than problem solve, to hug rather than teach.

It is also better to say nothing when your spouse feels overwhelmed and unable to overcome. The majority of people have had times when the world crowds in, everything is difficult, and darkness seems to envelop. Times when the silver lining, present in every cloud (as the old saying goes), has rusted away and is nowhere to be found. Times when the 'rain' seems to be persistently falling from the said cloud and is here to stay - for what seems like an indefinite time ahead.

Undoubtedly, you have experienced times like these, hopefully not too often. If you are like most other married couples, you have probably lived through periods when your 'significant' other is in a 'significant' funk and can't seem to 'snap out of it'. I know that Lainey hates it when I have times when I'm feeling down. Times like these are hard, not only for the funk-ee but also for both of you. Watching the one you love struggle, hurts. Their struggles, whether with life in general, depression or anxiety, are very real to them and it's painful to watch from the sidelines.

It's natural to want to help, to encourage them to "snap out of it", "pick themselves up", but often our well-meaning attempts bounce off a seemingly impenetrable barrier. Sometimes when you offer help, the ricochet is nothing more than a damp-squib comment devoid of emotion, other times it cuts and adds to the hurt. Failed attempts to fix the situation can cause a swing to the other extreme. Instead of trying to help, the default becomes leaving them to stew in their own juices or wallow in their own self-pity. This rarely goes well either.

So what does Lainey do when I behave like Eeyore? She desperately needs the ice to thaw and often it is this need, this desperation, that determines her words, attitude and actions. Since the driving force is emotional, it's rare that those words, attitudes and actions come over well. Instead of: encouragement, distraction, attempting to cheer-up, offering solutions or even going to extremes of presenting ultimatums; Lainey has found it more successful to shift the focus off her personal needs and onto what her 'beloved donkey' needs to feel human again.

You're probably asking if that's the case what works? The Bible says to carry one another's burdens (Galatians 6:2). This is not to say you should do everything for your spouse (Galatians 6:5 is quite clear about that). Everyone needs to carry their own load, fulfil their own responsibilities, but when the load becomes overwhelmingly burdensome it is right that you step in and help.

No one likes to be overburdened, no one wants to think that they are a burden to someone else either. For this reason, take care not to add to their feeling of helplessness by making them feel like an inconvenience. Instead, respond with empathy, it's impossible to communicate to the fullest degree without it. It's a vital tool in your communication tool belt.

So what is empathy? According to the Merriam Webster dictionary, empathy is defined as: 'the action of understanding, being aware of, being sensitive to, and vicariously experiencing the feelings, thoughts, and experience of another of either the past or present without having the feelings, thoughts, and experience fully communicated in an objectively explicit manner'. Without empathy you're unable to understand your spouse's emotions fully, you will be confined to hearing on an intellectual (or topical) level only, which significantly limits your ability to communicate.

Sympathy is totally different, while empathy allows us to feel with someone, sympathy is limited to only feeling for them. Sympathy is an awareness of the needs and feelings of others, seeing things from their point of view, and being able to feel for them. Empathy surpasses sympathy, in that it too stretches beyond a purely cognitive (or intellectual) understanding and could be described as feeling with somebody. Empathy is understanding to the degree that you feel what they are feeling.

Although it is your responsibility to carry one another's burdens (Galatians 6:2) you are not responsible for fixing their emotions. Only God can do that. God invites us to tell Him about our anxieties and give them over to Him.

> **Casting all your cares**
> **[all your anxieties, all your worries, and all your concerns,**
> **once and for all] on Him, for He cares about you**
> **[with deepest affection, and watches over you very carefully].**
> **1 Peter 5:7 AMP**

Now that you know what your responsibility is and what it isn't, it's easier to respond in a healthier way. Take time to ask how they are feeling, give them time to explore what is going on in their life and ask questions that help them understand what pressures they are experiencing. Ask them to imagine what would be happening around them in an environment where they felt less burdened. Once they've identified that encourage them to see what small steps they can take to move in that direction. Be careful not to offer solutions or fall into 'fix it' mode. Try to remember to ask rather than tell. That's not to say, having discovered the pressures, that you are forbidden from helping in some way. Help, where you can, to lift the load without your spouse feeling they have become the problem.

IMPORTANT! - The advice above is for those experiencing small road bumps rather than a serious medical condition. If your spouse has prolonged periods of depression, feels sad or hopeless every day for most of the day, or has spoken about suicidal thoughts, get immediate medical help. Depression is a serious medical condition and should not be dismissed as something that is of no consequence.

Over to You!

- *Have you ever offered your spouse unsolicited advice?*
  - *How did they respond?*
- *Do you have a tendency to fix the problem and ignore your spouse's feelings?*
  - *Do you tend to assume that your spouse is not able to correct issues that they experience? Is there any evidence for this?*
  - *Knowing that empathy is needed in your relationship, what can you do to make sure you don't come across as uncaring?*
- *Are you uncomfortable during times when your spouse is overwhelmed, and you are unable to make things better for them?*
  - *Are you able to recognise that empathy, although not fixing things, will help? If you are having trouble recognising this discuss it together.*
- *Have you been struggling with feeling low?*
  - *Reach out for help. Tell your spouse what you need.*
  - *Reach out to God. He cares about every emotion you have experienced and every tear you have shed.*

> **You keep track of all my sorrows.**
> **You have collected all my tears in your bottle.**
> **You have recorded each one in your book.**
> **Psalm 56:8 NLT**

#marriagetip

When you are struggling with keeping quiet, remember that you don't need to be quiet with God. He is never overwhelmed, never too busy to listen and is always there. He won't even be upset if you give Him unsolicited advice (although He will do what is right, not necessarily what you want).

When to Say Something

Refusing to communicate with your spouse is like starving your marriage of the oxygen it needs to breathe. It might be wrong to 'air your dirty laundry in public', but it needs to be aired between the two of you! Don't let unresolved issues smother your relationship because you refuse to talk about them. Saying nothing used to be my 'go to' when I was upset.

The absence of words did not enhance the atmosphere in our home. There were days with cold stares, and an icy atmosphere, the unspoken cause of our frigidity resounded within the four walls of our home as though we had had a screaming match. Our house echoed the silence, magnifying the dysfunction between us. Not that we realised it was dysfunctional we just accepted it as the way things were. The way we dealt with problems.

'We don't argue', we would boast to friends. 'We haven't had an argument in four and a half years of marriage ... not even when we were dating'. Neither of us realised that this was a lie. We didn't understand that silence itself could be a loud argument. We fully believed that our relationship was secure because we didn't fight, we thought it was healthy.

I remember standing in the kitchen breathing out a loud sigh and listening while the kitchen cupboard stopped reverberating on its hinges. It was then I started to reconsider my method of dealing with conflict. Was this really a healthy way to deal with being upset? It certainly wasn't working well. Neither of us wanted to admit we had a problem. Usually after a few days, one of us would start to 'de-ice' and the atmosphere would gradually warm again until we reached a 'friendly' temperature.

What were the silences about? I call them silences because one could hardly call them arguments. Arguments required the use of words. They could be about the small things left undone, the big things we needed to come into agreement about. They could be about how much help I was 'not' getting or about Roy reading the mail before he gave me a kiss. Silence is not harmless, silence is a weapon. Silence is sinister because it never allows the other person to know what the problem is; it is a guessing game which is not easy to win. Silence is also manipulative. The pressure of being 'sent to Coventry' creates a change in behaviour, but it also causes resentment.

The change came when we were 'tricked' into doing a marriage course. I don't know whether our friends knew there were issues or they just wanted us to fill up the group, but we reluctantly tagged along. I guess in our arrogance we really didn't have high expectations, we thought there wasn't too much to learn. We were wrong about that too! There was much to learn, we had deeply ingrained patterns of behaviour which needed to change, and we were given the tools to cause them to change. We knew it was essential to improve and reverse our destructive patterns.

The first time we spoke about things, the lid blew off the can, and yes, we really were confronted with a can of worms. The 'little' things which could have been dealt with so easily had grown out of all proportion and like some mutant species needed annihilation. The anger and frustration that had been bottling up over the years poured forth. The honesty felt good and bad at the same time. The air was clearing, but it was painful to learn the actual condition of our relationship.

After the silence was broken, we started to learn that it was better to talk than to be quiet. It was better to deal with the issues as they arose rather than sticking our heads in the sand hoping that they would go away. We also learned not to swing to the other side of the pendulum and replace silence with arguing. Angry words were no better than silence, but discussion usually brought great results, even though the journey was often painful. We learned that talking about the issues didn't threaten the relationship it strengthened it.

Now when it's cold in our home, it's because someone left the door open. Silence is no longer a welcome guest unless of course, it is that comfortable, cosy silence when we are snuggling on the couch. The more wedding anniversaries we celebrate, the more it qualifies us to say that talking more works.

Perhaps the silence that has taken over your home has nothing to do with a silent argument but more to do with a shut down in communication. Other things steal your attention, and whether it's talking to others more than your spouse, getting lost in a book or a game or the modern epidemic of phubbing, there is little communication between you. For those of you who haven't heard of the term 'phubbing' before here's the definition.

Phubbing: to ignore (a person or one's surroundings) when in a social situation by busying oneself with a phone or other mobile device.

Phubbing is a word that was non-existent before 2012. It is a word that was specifically created as part of an advertising campaign, but the concept of snubbing someone in favour of doing another task or giving something else your attention is not new. Before technology, hiding behind a newspaper, a book or a kitchen sink were avoidance techniques. Avoidance itself communicates a lot whether you realise it or not.

Avoidance and distraction are mechanisms which close down communication. The reasons for closing down communication can vary, and assumption can be dangerous. Let's look at some of the possibilities.

One reason people might stay silent is that they fear conflict. Not everyone has the same attitude or approach to conflict. You might be entirely comfortable with a disagreement while the thought of a dispute might feel like the world is ending for your spouse.

> 'COURAGE IS WHAT IT TAKES TO STAND UP AND SPEAK;
> COURAGE IS ALSO WHAT IT TAKES TO SIT DOWN AND LISTEN'.
> WINSTON CHURCHILL

It seems appropriate to quote Winston Churchill when addressing the topic of fear of conflict, perhaps that is because it too often resembles a war. Each spouse dresses in their favoured battle fatigues, getting ready to 'win' at any cost. It does take courage to address conflict, but if you really want to resolve it, you need to be brave, not only in speaking but also in listening.

Another reason why you or your spouse might stay silent is because of indifference. You might lack passion about the subject your spouse wants to discuss, so you adopt a 'do what you like' approach. On the one hand, this gives your spouse freedom to choose; on the other hand, if your spouse was making a bid to engage you in conversation, and you push it away, you could be sending a negative relational message.

We already talked about one of the primary reasons communication is necessary is to build a friendship. Friendship comes from being interested in what each other has to say, showing interest in their day and what they did. Talking about subjects that interest them but don't always interest you to the same degree is a step away from indifference. Asking about each other's day and giving each other more than an, 'it was fine' answer will build your relationship. If both of you are willing to do this, you might find you learn something new. A conversation shouldn't be only by one person's rules; it should be a joint venture of discovery. Don't miss that adventure by avoiding talking to each other.

We've also seen selfishness play a big part in silent homes. It's possible to decide to keep watching that TV programme, or keep on playing a computer game or do something else that's fun for you rather than spending time in conversation with your spouse. It's important to recognise that your spouse has needs too and one of those needs is to chat with you.

If your home isn't completely silent, but your communication has come down to a list of requests or instructions you are missing out. Don't behave like a teenager who is going through their monosyllable phase. Don't make conversation hard work because you want to get back to something that you want to do. If you work on your relationship it's not only your spouse who will reap the benefits, you will too! It's time to put away the selfishness and say something that will build your relationship.

Unfortunately, some of you who are reading this will be close to giving up trying. Has past experience made you feel that making an effort to communicate is hopeless? Perhaps you have felt unheard, misunderstood or hurt to name a few. It's difficult when you are wounded to try again. Being silent isn't helpful, it will continue to harm you if you bottle up your feelings and never speak about them.

Over to You!

- *Are there any times when you have been silent when you should have spoken?*
- *Have you found yourself avoiding saying anything? If so why?*
  - *Has a fear of conflict, indifference, selfishness or hopelessness played a part in that?*

- *Are there any other reasons why you sometimes don't speak when you should?*

• *Are you frustrated by the silence that comes from your spouse?*

- *Why do you think that silence is in place?*
- *Why not talk to them about it? Perhaps your assumptions are incorrect.*

#marriagetip

Some people struggle to share what they want to share unless they have it well planned out. Mark Twain once wrote 'It usually takes me more than three weeks to prepare a good impromptu speech'. It's not wrong to think things through beforehand, just be careful about running scenarios since it leads to guessing what your spouse might say or think.

Listening

Listening isn't a natural talent for many people. In fact, listening, like any other skill is something that needs practice. You might think that it's natural, you can hear, so you are good at listening, we wish that were true! Unfortunately, most people focus on the spoken part of communication and their listening skills could use a bit of work. When you take time to really listen you will discover that you start to understand your spouse on a whole new level. A key principle of listening is to listen with intent, listen to understand.

> **An intelligent heart acquires knowledge,**
> **and the ear of the wise seeks knowledge.**
> **Proverbs 18:15 ESV**

My father, Cecil, has lost a lot of his hearing, which means that he needs to wear hearing aids in both ears to hear anything. If they aren't working, then he relies on lip-reading. Dad has a rather cheeky sense of humour and has used his deafness to his advantage every now and again when Mum has been annoyed with him. His not so subtle action of reaching up to turn off his hearing aid has often resulted in laughter, but my dad isn't the only one guilty of selective hearing.

Over the years if we had been paid for each time someone has complained that their spouse doesn't listen to them, we would be rich. It seems that the art of listening has been lost, yet listening is as much a part of communication as speaking. If you've developed the habit of tuning out your spouse, then you're going to have to make a lot of effort to correct that. There is a leap between hearing someone (almost as background noise) and consciously registering what they are saying.

Using our imagination a little we can imagine the conversations this will spark, accusations could come all too quickly! Before you're tempted to accuse your spouse of not listening it might be worthwhile knowing why people develop selective hearing:

1. They tune out until something interesting is said then they tune back into the conversation. Our brains cope with peripheral noise by filtering out sounds to focus on what's most important. If you feel you're not being heard, then you've got to ask if you've got the timing right for the conversation. It's also possible that the person listening needs to decide to up the priority of what their spouse is saying to them.

2. They tune out as a coping mechanism. In the same way that people who live near a noisy road or a railway track tune out the noise, people adjust to the background track of their environment. For fourteen years Roy and I lived very close to a runway. When we first moved there we thought that the aircraft flying overhead were deafening. They were so loud that the windows would rattle in their frames, yet by the end of our time in Warton, we hardly noticed when one flew directly overhead. If you have the tendency to nag and monologue, then it's possible your spouse will resort to selective hearing to cope with the tirade.

Over to You!

- *Give yourself a score 1-10 (with 10 being the highest) on how good you are at listening. Then score your spouse. Compare scores to see if your answers match.*
- *When do you have a tendency to tune out your spouse?*
- *Why do you tune them out?*
- *What does it feel like when your spouse doesn't listen to you?*

#marriagetip

The first step to being heard is to listen. This might sound strange but getting louder and speaking over your spouse won't get you heard. You'll be heard when you start respecting each other's right to speak.

> THE ART OF CONVERSATION LIES IN LISTENING.
> MALCOM FORBES

Listen with the Right Attitude

The English idiom, 'I'm all ears' reflects a keenness to hear what the speaker has to say. It is usually used when someone is hoping to hear some gossip, or it's used in a sarcastic way when someone doesn't want to hear what their spouse is saying. There are certain subjects which send me to sleep. When these subjects come up, I'm not 'all ears' because I'm not interested and it is hard to fake that I am. In marriage, that means that some subjects interest Roy which simply don't interest me. He trained as an engineer, and he loves figuring out how things have been designed. At the start of our marriage, he would launch into lengthy explanations regarding technology, that I found it difficult to engage in. Equally, Roy would zone out whenever I talked about English literature. The bottom line is that not every subject is going to interest your spouse and those differences don't make them bad, uncaring or indifferent. Conversations should connect you rather than make you feel disconnected.

Roy still sometimes talks about things that are technical, but he has learned to read the signals indicating when he's diving in too deep. I love the fact that he gets animated when he is talking about things that interest him and that he gives me a window into that part of his life. Understanding his thoughts and feelings brings a sense of closeness because I am learning more about him, who he is as a person and how he has been designed.

I'm blessed that Roy has been willing to let me chat about English literature, he's even gone to see a play or two with me! However, like Roy, I've developed sensitivity regarding how long those conversations are or how deeply we discuss the topic. We don't just talk to tell the other what we know but rather to share who we are with one another.

> We have two ears and one mouth so
> that we can listen twice as much as we speak.
> Epictetus

Over to You!

- Are you listening with the right attitude?

- Do you listen to try and understand your spouse rather than the subject they're talking about?

- Are you sensitive to your spouse's needs when you are talking about a subject you feel passionately about?

    - Do you know when to stop talking?

    - Do you know when to switch topics?

- Are you listening twice as much as you speak or speaking twice as much as you listen?

#marriagetip

We have both learned, over the years, to let go of our own selfish desire to speak only about topics which are of direct interest to us individually. It's amazing what you can learn when you take the time to listen to each other. If you're guilty of taking up most of the 'air time' then you might be missing out on the opportunity of really knowing and understanding your spouse. If your spouse is on the quieter side, don't feel the need to jump in and fill the silence, give them time to speak!

Listen by Looking

When a woman is speaking to you, listen to what she says with her eyes.
Victor Hugo

I have noticed that when I am in a classroom full of children if I want to get their attention, I often say "Look at me" rather than "Listen to me". Once they make eye contact, I feel like I have their full attention and will then say what I need to communicate. I'm not sure where this habit originates, although I did work in a deaf school for a few years and that may be where I picked it up. That experience taught me to pay attention to what the person is saying, not only with their words (or signs) but with their facial expressions and body language.

I have a deep sense that if someone isn't looking at me when I speak that they are not listening, and that includes my husband. I don't like having a conversation with Roy if he is working at his computer, reading a book, watching T.V. or looking at his phone. I would rather wait until he can listen, rather than speak to him without getting a response. You may have assumed that when Roy is involved in any one of those activities that he rudely ignores me and doesn't respond, actually nothing could be further from the truth. Roy usually answers when I ask something, and if he can't give me his immediate attention will say something like, "Wait a minute honey, I just need to finish this." and then he gives me an answer. With that being the case why don't I feel like Roy is listening? One reason why, is that he doesn't respond to me in a way which indicates to me that he is listening. My cultural 'ears' and his are two very different things.

To gain a clearer understanding of what is considered to be listening in your personal culture, you can ask yourself a few questions:

1. What do you expect an active listener to do in order to indicate that they are listening? It might be to turn to you, make eye contact, echo back, give an encouraging response or stop their work for a moment.

2. In your spouse's personal culture, what is expected from an active listener in order to indicate that they are listening? Are they the same things or are they different from yours?

I have to admit to being reluctant to make any suggestions about what might be indicators of attentive listening. Don't get stuck on those that are listed here. Think about your home life and what is integral to it. In some cultures looking at someone eye to eye is rude and yet in others, it is a polite way to acknowledge that you are interested in what the other person is talking about. Body language communicates interest or disinterest too, so are you listening well?

If you have grown up in a home where the communication between your parents has been poor; some bad habits may have rubbed off on you. You will need to work together to establish good patterns which communicate to your spouse that you are present, you are interested, and you are listening. That means moving from a passive stance on listening to becoming actively engaged. If you continue to listen the way you've always listened you will not move to true communication. Remember, communication is only successful when someone receives the same intellectual and emotional message that the other person intended. To receive that message you need to listen actively.

Culture isn't the only factor to affect our listening habits, gender differences will inevitably impact what is considered to be listening too. In fact, many women will accuse men of never listening, but men would level the same charge against the women in their life. The point is that most people struggle to listen and science reveals that only 25 percent of our listening skills could be deemed effective.[13]

---

[13]   The Listening Course. Tracey Service. www.thelisteningcourse.com

The reason why women think men don't listen and men think women don't either is a little more complicated. When we listen there is usually an active response, that response is often the nod of a head or a verbal interjection, but did you know that men and women don't use these tools in the same way? Women will nod, say 'mm-hmmm' or 'ah-huh' because they are indicating that they are listening and want their spouse to keep on talking. The problem is that when a man hears these responses, he hears agreement! Men tend to use those types of responses <u>only</u> when they agree with what is being said.

This may explain why so many men feel that they have their wife's agreement and are confused when they discover they don't. It also provides a rational explanation as to why women often feel men don't really want to hear what they have to say. They don't feel as encouraged during the conversation because they misinterpret their spouse's lack of verbal 'encouragers' as disinterest.

Over to You!

- *How much eye contact do you give your spouse when you are listening?*
- *What do you need your spouse to do so that you know they are listening?*
- *What do you need to do to show your spouse that you are listening?*
- *Have you picked up any bad/good habits from the way your parents communicated?*
- *Were you surprised by anything you learnt in this section?*
  - *If so, what was new?*
  - *How do you think it will affect your communication?*

#marriagetip

Focus on what you can do to help your spouse know that you are listening. Make sure you communicate, in a constructive way, what you need in order to feel heard.

Listen Without Interrupting

"I have a confession to make", announced one of my uncles who was making a speech at our wedding. "I haven't spoken to my wife in years", he said with a downcast expression. An audible hush came over everyone, and many looked shocked. His timing was perfect, and without missing a beat, he looked up then grinned and declared, "I couldn't bear to interrupt her!" Laughter erupted, and the wedding jokes continued.

Both genders can get annoyed when they are sharing their heart and they get interrupted. If you don't like to be interrupted when you speak, bear that in mind when your spouse is talking. While you might interpret your own interruption as a show of interest or encouragement, you probably doubt your spouse's motives when they do the same. If you hear statements like, 'You always interrupt' or 'You never listen' then try and make some changes. Although if you're the one making those accusations you should stop and assess if that's actually true, are you making generalisations rather than being fair?

> No one is as deaf as the man who will not listen.
> Yiddish Proverb

We've witnessed a lot of situations when a couple 'talk over' one another. They can't possibly hear what their spouse is saying because they are too busy making their point. 'Talking over' each other is deeply ingrained in some cultures.

Listening without interrupting is hugely difficult for those who feel the need to fight their corner. When a communication pattern has been destructive, the aim of communication changes from understanding and being understood. In order to be heard the voices get louder and stronger and faster. The point becomes winning the argument, but in doing so you can lose the battle for your relationship.

> **A fool takes no pleasure in understanding,**
> **but only in expressing his opinion.**
> **Proverbs 18:2 ESV**

Proverbs doesn't pull any punches when it describes a person who resorts to this type of communication.

If one gives an answer before he hears, it is his folly and shame.
Proverbs 18:13 ESV

One of our favourite videos on YouTube is a simple sketch entitled 'It's not about the nail'. A husband is struggling to listen to his wife, he tries to sit patiently as he hears her explain her situation and the areas in which she is experiencing pain. All the while he can see a nail sticking out of her forehead and all he wants to do is to take it out so that she can feel better.

Listening patiently isn't easy, especially if you've been hard-wired to try and discover the problem and find a solution quickly. The solution is actually to be still, to listen to attempt to understand and help your spouse feel understood. Women are much more able to deal with the world around them and solve the issues that come their way when they have been able to express their emotions first. That means that you might have to wait to disclose your opinion, but it will be worth it!

> **Whoever is patient has great understanding,**
> **but one who is quick-tempered displays folly.**
> **Proverbs 14:29 NIV**

Both men and women desire to be heard, but they signal they are listening in different ways. So how do you prove that you're listening attentively? One effective way of demonstrating that you're listening is to paraphrase to show understanding. It's like holding up a mirror and reflecting back what you heard. It's clarifying that you have understood at a deeper level and that the picture you have is the same as the one they intended to communicate. This is a skill that counsellors develop, but it isn't something that most couples put into practice.

OVER TO YOU!

- *Do you find it difficult to listen without interrupting?*
- *How do you feel when your spouse interrupts you?*
- *Are you guilty of talking over one another?*
- *How patient are you when your spouse is speaking to you?*
    - *Are you patient to listen, and are you patient when you are interrupted?*

#marriagetip

Remember that listen and silent are spelt with the same letters. You need to be quiet while your spouse is sharing, then reflect back what you've heard to check understanding.

Throughout this book you've read about a lot of principles regarding improving your communication, it really is a vast subject! Some principles you will have already tried to put into practice, others you might still be trying to get your head around. Be patient with yourself and your spouse as you practice communication. It takes time, energy and plenty of practice to adopt these principles and create the communication patterns you desire. Practice makes permanent so don't get discouraged when you fall back into old and familiar modes of communication. Rather, learn from your mistakes and start putting the principles back in place. With time, you will be able to improve the communication and connection between you both.

Now it's really Over to You!

Use the space below to record the things you know you need to focus on improving the most.

>Love is patient, love is kind.
>It does not envy, it does not boast, it is not proud.
>1 Corinthians 13:4 NIV

Other books by Hitched

BY LAINEY HITCHMAN

by Roy & Lainey Hitchman

Coming Soon

By Roy & Lainey Hitchman

Also Available

Bibliography

BOOKS

Chapman Gary. The Five Love Languages

Emerson Eggerichs, Love & Respect: The Love She Most Desires; The Respect He Desperately Needs

Gottman John. The Seven Principles for Making Marriage Work

Lee, Nicky & Sila. The Marriage Book

Love Patricia, Stosney Steven. Why Women Talk and Men Walk

Oden, Thomas. Care of Souls in the Classic Tradition. Philadelphia, PA: Fortress, 1984

Parton Steven. The Science of Happiness: Why complaining is literally killing you

Tannen Deborah: You Just Don't Understand Women and Men in Conversation

The Body Language Project. The Only Book on Body Language That Everyone Needs to Read

ARTICLES and PERIODICALS

The Four Horsemen
https://www.gottman.com/blog/the-four-horsemen-contempt/

Leadership for Life – What We're Made of | Workforce http://workforcesolutions.stlcc.edu/2014/leadership-for-life-what-were-made-of/

The Ladder of Inference
http://www.skillsyouneed.com/ips/ladder-of-inference.html

6 Ways Men and Women Communicate Differently
https://psychcentral.com/blog/6-ways-men-and-women-communicate-differently/

Brain Differences Between the Genders
https://www.psychologytoday.com/intl/blog/hope-relation-
ships/201402/

Can Screaming Be Bad for Your Relationship
https://www.psychologytoday.com/blog/what-would-aristotle-
do/201508/can-screaming-or-yelling-be-bad-your-relationship

The Difference Between a Dialogue and a Monologue
https://www.psychologytoday.com/au/blog/the-novel-perspec-
tive/201201/the-difference-between-monologue-and-dialogue

Dobson, Dr James C. Enjoy Greater Intimacy in Your Marriage
http://salemnet.vo.llnwd.net/o29/promotions/mft/intimacy.pdf

BIOGRAPHY

Roy and Lainey Hitchman met at university in the late 80's. Roy was studying aeronautical engineering and was on the university rowing team. Lainey was studying English and had a love of coffee. They got married during their student years, and God started to stir their hearts to help people navigate their relationships.

They have been ministering to families since 1993. Their passion for working with relationships led to them founding a ministry called 'Hitched' which encompasses working with a wide variety of relationships through a number of stages in life. Roy and Lainey share hard-hitting yet life-giving principles through transparency and humour.

Roy and Lainey spend much of their time speaking, writing and reaching out to those who need some encouragement in the area of relationships. When they aren't travelling, they enjoy spending time with their family, Ryan, Beth, Erin and their son-in-law Jonathan although it takes a little organisation to get everyone in one place at one time.

If you would like to learn more about their ministry, find more resources or get in touch you can contact them through www.hitchedtogether.com or www.lifeforsingles.com. If you would like them to speak at your church, seminar or conference, then please contact them via email at info@hitchedtogether.com

www.ingramcontent.com/pod-product-compliance
Lightning Source LLC
Chambersburg PA
CBHW071342080526
44587CB00017B/2926